Christopher Matthew is the author of *Now We Are Sixty*, *Now We Are Sixty (And a Bit)*, *Summoned by Balls* and *The Old Man and the Knee*. He lives in London and Suffolk.

Also by Christopher Matthew

A Different World: Stories of Great Hotels
The Long-Haired Boy
Three Men in a Boat (annotated edition with Benny Green)
The Junket Man
How to Survive Middle Age
The Amber Room
A Nightingale Sang in Fernhurst Road
Now We Are Sixty
Now We Are Sixty (And a Bit)
Summoned by Balls
When We Were Fifty
The Man Who Dropped the Le Creuset on His Toe
and Other Bourgeois Mishaps
Dog Treats: An Assortment of Mutts, Mongrels,
Puppies and Pooches
A Bus Pass Named Desire: Romances for the Young at Heart
The Old Man and the Knee: How to Be a Golden Oldie

THE SIMON CRISP DIARIES

Diary of a Somebody
Loosely Engaged
The Crisp Report
Family Matters
Knocking On

A TRIPLE-DECKER TREAT

Collected Poems for Old Dogs and Young Hearts

CHRISTOPHER MATTHEW
Illustrations by Tony Ross

ABACUS

First published in Great Britain in 2019 by Abacus

1 3 5 7 9 10 8 6 4 2

Copyright © Christopher Matthew 2013, 2014, 2016
Collection Copyright Christopher Matthew 2019
Illustrations Copyright Tony Ross 2013, 2014, 2016

The moral right of the author has been asserted.

*All characters and events in this publication, other than those
clearly in the public domain, are fictitious and any resemblance
to real persons, living or dead, is purely coincidental.*

All rights reserved.
No part of this publication may be reproduced, stored in a
retrieval system, or transmitted, in any form or by any means, without
the prior permission in writing of the publisher, nor be otherwise circulated
in any form of binding or cover other than that in which it is published
and without a similar condition including this condition being
imposed on the subsequent purchaser.

A CIP catalogue record for this book
is available from the British Library.

ISBN 978-1-4087-1013-5

Typeset in Minion by M Rules
Printed and bound in Great Britain by Clays Ltd, Elcograf S.p.A.

Papers used by Abacus are from well-managed forests
and other responsible sources.

Abacus
An imprint of
Little, Brown Book Group
Carmelite House
50 Victoria Embankment
London EC4Y 0DZ

An Hachette UK Company
www.hachette.co.uk

www.littlebrown.co.uk

A TRIPLE-DECKER TREAT

Contents

The Man Who Dropped the Le Creuset on His Toe and Other Bourgeois Mishaps

Dog Treats: An Assortment of Mutts, Mongrels, Puppies and Pooches

A Bus Pass Named Desire: Romances for the Young at Heart

The Man Who Dropped the Le Creuset on His Toe and Other Bourgeois Mishaps

Introduction

Accidents are nearly always idiotic, and sometimes positively bizarre. Normally unavoidable, they catch even the wariest of us at the most unlikely moments. However sensibly, or intelligently, or carefully we pick our way through the hither and yon of daily life, something is often waiting to bring us up in our tracks – be it the lamp-post one walks into while looking the other way, the garden rake that lies upright, waiting for the misplaced boot, or the panic attack that induces the normally level-headed men to curtsey to the Duke of Edinburgh.

P. G. Wodehouse put it down to pure fate, which, 'if it slips us a bit of goose with one hand, is pretty sure to give us the sleeve across the windpipe with the other.'

The English middle classes are, on the whole, treated to more good luck than most. Indeed, they often feel it to be their entitlement; so that when something unexpected happens to shake them out of their routine of complacency, it comes as a much greater shock than it might to those for whom life is altogether more grim and earnest.

I have still to recover from the moment in March 2010 when, having eased myself out of a chair lift in a Swiss ski resort – something I had been doing man and boy without any problems for over sixty years – I stumbled, fell sideways into a pile of snow and broke my hip.

Undergoing the operation (while awake, I might say), spending weeks with crutches, a walking stick and physiotherapy wasn't half as much fun as telling people about it. The more I told the story, the more I embellished it, until it began to take on the semblance – not to say the length – of a stand-up routine at the Hammersmith Apollo.

People enjoy hearing about other people's accidents – the more exotic and idiotic the better. Those who have had a similar experience are relieved to know they are not alone; those who have not are happy in their mistaken assumption that nothing as silly as that can happen to them.

I myself experienced this blissful sense of *schadenfreude* when describing my hip adventures to my editor, Richard Beswick, and he, having listened sympathetically, announced that he had recently dropped a Le Creuset casserole on his toe.

I didn't mean to laugh. In fact, my first reaction was to wince. However, the name Le Creuset added unexpected humour to the story – quite undeserved on Richard's part, since his toe was beginning to turn black and he would probably lose the nail, if not the entire toe.

On the other hand, the inclusion of the brand name immediately summed up the world in which cast-iron casseroles and other expensive kitchenware are part of the everyday landscape, and their owners should know better than to drop them on their toes. It was a classic bourgeois mishap, or middle-class disaster.

So too, I hope, are the cock-ups, catastrophes, calamities

and cataclysms described in the collection of comic, if at times wince-making, verses contained in this slim volume.

Some really happened to people I know, others to people who know the people they happened to, and some are just plain made up.

And, since you ask, my hip is better than it was, but still a bit stiff after I've been sitting. Like now, for example.

Christopher Matthew
London, November 2013

Trolleyed

Grizelda was a happy soul,
As kind as she was jolly,
Until the day she lost control,
Pushing a Waitrose trolley.

She shot between the fruit and veg,
Like someone on the Cresta
Aboard a disobedient sledge.
This all took place in Leicester.

Competitive Dad

A prat-in-chief was Charlie Plank –
A fellow born to brag and swank.
But worse still was his urge to win
Against his junior kith and kin.
Whatever any child could do,
He'd prove that he could do it, too –
And not just do it, do it better
In Lycra shorts or chunky sweater.

By his account, he was a man
Who'd been a true Olympian.
In his time he had faced the best
(Including Seb Coe in a vest).
He'd fenced at Cambridge, boxed there too,
And would have got a rowing blue,
But caught a crab just near Barnes Bridge
When bitten by a giant midge,
And lost his place to dear old Hugh
(That friend of Stephen You Know Who),
A story he was very fond
Of telling at the boating pond,
Where not one child could win a race
With Daddy rowing at full pace.

He'd make his youngest look a fool
In swimming galas at the pool
By seemingly to be all heart
And giving him a ten-yard start,
Then underlining adult strength
By thrashing him by half a length.

He really was a frightful pill;
He'd beat all three by thirty nil
In soccer contests in the park
That dragged on well into the dark.
His batting skills were in no doubt;
He once made two-two-eight not out.

There was one sport where they excelled:
Their skiing was unparalleled –
The simple reason being they
Had started young in old Saas-Fee;
And being so close to the snow
They'd ski as fast as they could go.
Not having very far to fall,
They hadn't any fear at all.

Now Charles was nearly thirty-eight
When he had learnt to ski (and skate) –
The same time as his cool young brood,
Though in a slightly grumpy mood
When relegated to a group
Of older types – a cautious troupe
Who took their time with gentle turns
And lots of cream on lots of burns.

Still, Charlie saw no reason why
He should not keep up with his fry;
So, after lunch (and full of wine)
He'd set off with the little swine.
The faster that they went, he'd go
Careering wildly through the snow,
Determined to be at the front,
Despite the odd disastrous shunt
That left him sprawling on his face –
A faller in snow's steeplechase.

One day while heading off to lunch,
They happened on a cheerful bunch
Of local children doing jumps
On fairly simple, rough-hewn bumps,
And, dauntless in the frosty air,
Were showing off their freestyle flair
With flips and twists and spins and kicks,
Plus several ad hoc hotdog tricks.

The boys could only stand and stare;
They knew that they could never dare
To beat the locals at their game,
And Dad, of course, was far too lame ...

'Wow! That looks fun!' they hear him cry.
'Come on, chaps, let's all have a try!'
They hang their heads and look away;
Next thing they know, he's under way,
With legs spread wide and arms akimbo,
Their father's floating by in limbo ...

He broke his hip, his pelvis too,
A tibia, a rib or two,
And, helmetless, he bashed his head,
And, sad to say, he's now stone dead.

A gravestone tells the sorry tale
Of this most tragic alpha male.
It's written there beneath his name:
WHATE'ER THE ODDS, HE WON THE GAME.

The Shaming of Anthea Sims

Our pub quiz team is one bod short
Since Anthea Sims was one day caught
Alone inside the ladies' loo
In serious chat with who knows who,
With BlackBerry attached to ear
And whispering, 'I can't quite hear.
Was that Leif Ericson you said,
The son of whatsisname, The Red?'

When challenged by the opposition,
She claimed a mild indisposition.
'I've had some trouble with my bowels,'
She said in well-bred, cut-glass vowels.
'I wouldn't want it spread around;
You know how things like this rebound.
Next thing I'll hear I'm at death's door!
I didn't want to be a bore;
I thought I'd ring the surgery ...
I swear this isn't perjury ...
My doctor's name is Ericson,
Which, as you know, means Eric's son ...
His father was a Communist,
A well-known gynaecologist,
Known fondly as "The Red" by mums,
And some of us have stayed good chums ...
He's ninety now and very spry,
And living on the Isle of Skye ...

She rambled on, but all in vain;
She sounded more and more insane.
The game was up; she knew it, too.
There was nothing she could do
But stand there as if in a trance;
She wouldn't get a second chance.

She had to go; she knew the rules;
She couldn't take us *all* for fools.

Her eyes welled up; she shed a tear;
She didn't stop to drink her beer;
She stumbled out, sad sight indeed –
A salted snail in oatmeal tweed.

We haven't won a quiz night since;
Our scores would make a schoolboy wince;
While Anthea, you'll be pleased to find,
Is doing well on *Mastermind* –
At home, with all her reference books,
And no one there to give dark looks.

Builders' Last Laugh

I've got this foreign builder chap,
A nice young man called Fred.
I can't tell by his accent,
But I think he's quite well bred.

We always have a lot of laughs;
He's now a kind of friend.
He couldn't be more helpful, but
He drives me round the bend.

I bought some instant Carte Noire
(From Waitrose, since you ask:
I challenge anyone to say
I cannot multi-task.)

One does one's best to get on terms
With builders and the like,
But … well … as far as they're concerned,
We lot can take a hike.

He never even touched the stuff,
Preferring, so I glean,
Nespresso macchiato
From our spanking new machine.

I didn't like to mention it;
One doesn't like to fuss.
One's dealings with one's builders
Are invariably thus.

Last week I came home early and
There, slumbering in our bed
Was Joachim the plasterer,
And, next to him, young Fred.

Tragedia Toscana

The doyens of Chiantishire
Were Jill and Johnny Uthwatt-Burr.
The couple had a yen to roam,
But Tuscany's their home from home –
To be precise, near Montalcino,
Where they enjoyed an annual beano
Of gastro outings there and here
To recommended *trattorie*.

The five-star choice in all the books
Was owned by Aldo – 'Cook of Cooks'.
Il Gamberetto was its name,
And such its fast-expanding fame
That it could take three months or more
To get one's foot inside the door.

The Uthwatt-Burrs pulled every string,
But nothing that they did could swing
A booking on their last night there.
Dear God! They simply couldn't bear
To think of eating *en famille*
Instead of one last gastro spree.

But good will come to those who wait,
And shortly after ten to eight
A man called from the restaurant
To say that if they came along,
A cock-up by the *maître d'*
Had left a corner table free.

The couple didn't pause to think;
They chucked the meat sauce in the sink,
And sprinted to the hired Fiat,
Triumphant that at last they'd be at
One of *the* great seafood joints,
Which in their foodie eyes meant POINTS.

John gave the little car full power
And got there in just half an hour ...

The Soave vanished down their gullets;
The waiter brought their grilled red mullets.
John smacked his lips; he took a bite.
Jill's eyes popped out; her face turned white.
She said, 'Oh bollocks! What an ass!
I've left our pasta on the gas!'

The walls turned black, the gas stove burst.
At least they ate their dinner first.

Boden Man

Zak's father, hot and sweaty,
In cargo shorts and specs,
Leapt smugly off a jetty,
Displaying well-formed pecs.

They found him quite soon after;
'Oh no!' they heard him shout.
He couldn't have looked dafter;
The ruddy tide was out.

Boogie Frights

Elizabeth and Rupert Gore
Were magic on the ballroom floor.
The quickstep was their claim to fame:
Unbeatable when on their game,
They'd won some prizes as a pair
At local dances here and there.
In Spain they cleaned up with a tango,
Which shows the way that these things can go.

Once, on a cruise, they cut a rug
And triumphed with a jitterbug,
And concentrated thence on disco –
A skill they honed in San Francisco.
Their *pièce de* was gangnam style:
They stood out by a country mile
From amateurs who 'did their thing',
With all the tripe that that can bring.

At forty-five they hit their peak
In Haslemere in Easter Week
At Boo and Henry's wedding bash,
Where, after dins, they cut a dash
So lively that the bride and groom
(And virtually half the room)
Stood there in silence, mouths ajar,
Like pop fans with a superstar.

Two teenagers were standing near;
One said out loud, so all could hear,
'It's sad to see the elderly
Pretending to be you and me.
If only they would act their age.
They're too old to take centre stage.'

They never hit the floor again
In England, France, or on the main.
These days they live in Argentina
(A much more tolerant arena),
And tango till their arches fall,
And no one laughs at them at all.

The Man Who Dropped the Le Creuset on His Toe

There was a chap whose name was Rick;
His children sometimes called him Dick
Behind his back, unlike his wife –
Mind you, she had a stressful life.

Being a perfectionist,
She drove her husband round the twist.

Their house in Bourton-on-the-Water
Was heaven on earth – a real ripsnorter.
Nicky Haslam, Tricia Guild,
Colefax, Fowler, nicely chilled,

And being such a decent egg,
It cost poor Rick an arm and leg.

Her kitchen was her pride and joy:
Equipped with every trick and toy,
It had a cosy farmhouse look –
A rocking chair, an inglenook,
And just a hint of sex appeal
With fabrics dyed in cochineal,
And every surface clean and bare –
No sign of clutter anywhere.

Her maxim was that less means more;
Hence every cupboard, every drawer
Was filled with trendy kitchenware
Of every shape and size, I swear.
And some you wouldn't think exist –
Not even on a wedding list.

An Eva Solo Citrus Squeezer;
Zabaglione pans from Pisa;
Alessi electronic scales;
Nantucket Seafood plates for snails;

A set of Kai Wasabi knives;
A small machine for chopping chives;
A Jasper Conran salad bowl –
A hoard of gastro rock 'n' roll.

Now Rick was quite a helpful chap,
And when he thought the time was ripe,
He'd do a spot of washing up,
But chances were he'd break a cup.

He'd undertake the simplest task;
He wouldn't say, he'd never ask,
And sent his wife completely mad;
His kids would smirk and murmur 'Da-a-ad.'

Undaunted, he would drive her gaga
By cooking on the gas-fired Aga.
One day he tried a Sunday roast –
The poor lamb ended up as toast.

His wife in desperation banned
Him from the kitchen, raised her hand
And said (with quite unusual force),
'One more false move and it's divorce!'

But Rick was not a man to quail,
Or wail, or pale, or rail, or fail.
He'd give his wife a nice surprise,
And be a hero in her eyes.

A stew, he felt, would hit the spot –
A simple dish, but good and hot,
With meat and veg and spuds and wine –
A blend of Oliver and Stein,

With just a hint of Eastern spice –
The sort Koreans find quite nice.
A *tang* perhaps, or maybe *guk*,
As per her Eastern cookery book.

He settled on a dish from Seoul
And fetched the biggest casserole –
Volcanic red by You-Know-Who,
Cast iron, natch, for perfect stew.

He grabs Le Creuset with both hands,
He trips, it falls, and promptly lands –
Oh, wretched fate; oh, cruel blow –
Slap, bang upon his big right toe.

The nail went black, infection came.
He said, 'I'm really not to blame.'
The children groaned, 'You shouldn't try, Dad.'
His life was one long jeremiad;
And when he had his toe removed,
His wife was, frankly, quite unmoved.
She said, 'Well, what can you expect?
You have no skills in this respect.
Mind you, it worked out on the whole;
You could have smashed the Conran bowl.'

Belinda Brown, Who Logged Out in No Uncertain Terms

Belinda Brown was no one's fool –
The brightest of the bright at school;
A polymath of deep conviction,
And yet a well of contradiction.
The owner of a doctorate;
Computer-wise – illiterate.

For reasons she could not explain,
She bought a ticket (to Bahrain) –
Not through her travel agent, Brett,
But online via the internet.
Again, for reasons inexplicable,
She filled in something inapplicable.
Convinced she'd failed, she tried once more,
And now was absolutely sure
She'd coughed up twice. *But how to check?*
It drove her mad, she was a wreck.

A nervous breakdown followed fast;
The trouble was, it never passed.
And now she lives in North Tibet,
Enraptured by the internet

Arrest Ye Merry

Tom Balls was a contrarian –
A smooth-faced, yet quite hairy man.
Religion was a case in point;
His faith was badly out of joint.
In empty churches quite devout,
In full ones much beset by doubt.
But once a year on Christmas Eve
He did his utmost to believe,
Upon his knees around midnight,
Comforted by candlelight.

But hard as Thomas tried to pray,
Attention would too often stray.

One Christmas, hot foot from the pub
(And feeling, frankly, somewhat sub),
Tom casually glanced along the pew
And saw a blonde girl dressed in blue,
Who bore a likeness, very slightly,
To Tom's great heart throb, Keira Knightley.

While murmuring the Gloria,
Transported by euphoria,
He stole a glance. She looked straight back.
He nearly had a cardiac.
She smiled. He felt his face go red.
Instead of God, he thought of bed,
And, at the altar on cloud nine,
He swallowed half a cup of wine.

His legs were weak; his arms the same;
His head was light; he felt no shame.
He stumbled back along the aisle,
His face fixed in a silly smile.
He knelt and bowed his head in prayer:
'Dear Lord,' he said, 'I know you're fair.
You don't do deals, I know that much,
And this is not an ask, as such,
But one kind word from Keira there,
And I'll rejoin the fold, I swear.'

He mingled with the crowd outside,
While trying to look dignified,
But of the girl there was no sign.
He had a word with Caroline,
The vicar, and drove home to bed,
Rather wishing he was dead.

He hadn't travelled very far
When, flagged down by a panda car,
He failed a breathalyser test,
And felt decidedly unblessed.

He's not first man to be shocked
That God is never lightly mocked.

Mary, Who Gave Up Well-Tuned Glutes
for Well-Turned Prose

One way to cure a wobbly arse
Is join a small Pilates class.
It sorts your abs, your hips, your thighs,
And frequently can lower size
From eighteen-plus to under ten,
And make you feel yourself again.

Now Mary Slim (ill-suited name
For such a fatty, such a shame)
Each Tuesday morning, fresh and bright
(With joints and muscles fairly tight),
Would take her mat and pink toe socks,
Her water and three lightweight blocks,
And rush off to the local gym
To shake a leg and stretch a limb
On Tower Trainer, Cadillac
And Ladder Barrel (brown and black).
Then, following this weekly grind,
She'd join her ladies and unwind
With skinny lattes, herbal teas,
And chew the fat and shoot the breeze.

But long, lean legs and firm, flat tum,
And well-toned abs and slinky bum
Were not to be for Mary Slim.
Her life, for her, was looking grim.
Despite her efforts on the mat,
She stayed unwaveringly fat.

Her spirits drooped, her midriff too.
'Why can't I do what others do?'
She wailed. 'My pelvis and my spine
Are nicely flexed and well in line,
But, bum-wise, I'm still Rubenesque –
A freak of nature, a grotesque.'

'I like you just the way you are,'
Her husband told her in the car.
'To tell the truth, these pecs and abs
Give me the serious abdabs.'

But no girl can be satisfied
Whose bottom measures six feet wide,
When all their fellow Pilatees
Are Katie Moss-like, if you please.

Now Mary was like one possessed
(Though keep-fit types are all obsessed).
She bought her own Deluxe Trapeze
And went at it like Herakles
Against the lion of Nemea,
Without an ounce of doubt or fear.

But, sad to say, this lion won,
And Mary at long last was done.
Her bum was her Achilles heel;
Though how it brought her down, I feel,
I'd rather not divulge right now;
Suffice to say, a pregnant cow
Could not have made a louder din
Than Mary, when they took her in;
And nurses of huge strength and skill
With training from Stoke Mandeville
Spent ages trying to untangle
Poor Mary's limbs from every angle.

She sold all her Pilates gear,
Half price, to Di who lived quite near,
And joined a local reading group –
A cosy, unambitious troupe,
For whom the latest P. D. James
Is worth a million slim-tone frames.

Chilling Out

A long weekend in Devon
For Julian and Fee
Was somewhat less than heaven,
They couldn't but agree.

The hotel was perfection,
The food the best by far;
But a serious objection
Was the rubbish mini-bar.

A nightcap after dinner
Would end a magic day;
But all that they had in there
Was a middling Chardonnay.

Basket Case

A pompous man was 'Sunny' Jim,
And, frankly, he was rather dim.
Four undistinguished years at Stowe
Meant he had nowhere else to go
But in the Church or in a bank,
Or in the army in a tank.
In fact, he had a dull career:
A humdrum Royal Engineer.
A major, it is true to say,
But not a type who made his way.
A decade's worth of selling soap
Had followed, but with little hope
Of making something of his life,
Or landing a half-decent wife.

And so he'd spent his latter years
Annoying people, bending ears,
Correcting grammar, picking holes
In politicians, scoring goals
In pointless, idiotic fights
With parking wardens, Labourites,
Nice ladies with their lollipops,
Young men with shaven heads in shops.
The tiniest whisper of a scrap,
He'd find it hard to shut his trap.
He'd argue morning, noon and night,
Convinced that he was always right.

For him there was no greater crime
Than wasting energy and time
In cluttered aisles and checkout lines
Of twerpish, half-baked philistines –
Their trolleys piled with special deals
On Heinz baked beans and ten-quid meals.
He'd fill a basket with the speed
Of starlings on a field of seed,
Then head unerringly for where
The shortest queue was he could bear.
One in particular he'd choose
(Except when stocking up with booze),
Reserved for those with special need –
i.e. a single mouth to feed.
One day he found himself alone
With perky checkout lady, Joan.
He counted out his meagre fare;
The sign above was clear as clear.

'A loaf of multi-seeded bread;
A mini-jar of salmon spread;
A guacamole dip (one scoop);
A tin of cock-a-leekie soup;
A dozen eggs. Five items, yes?
No problem there. No sweat. No stress.'
He dropped his voice to sound benign
And pointed upwards at the sign –
'Misuse of English gets my goat;
Forgive me, just a tiny note:
Merely a matter of finesse,
It should read FEWER there, not LESS.'

The checkout girl said, 'Thank you, sir.
I'd be quite happy to concur,
Except you've got six items here.
You've chosen the wrong queue, I fear.'

Her colleague came; a row broke out;
And Jim, as per, began to shout.
The manager was very nice:
'Two boxes of six eggs count twice,'
He said. 'The best thing you can do
Is join a proper, full-length queue.'

An hour later Jim emerged,
His sense of outrage still unpurged,
And set off in the murk and damp
To find his car had got a clamp.

Now coronaries can change a chap
As quickly as a thunderclap;
And Jim lay calmly on the ground
While paramedics bustled round.
A stoic air suffused his face
As IV lines were put in place,
And reassuring things were said,
And pillows placed around his head.
But Jim was made of sterner stuff,
And very soon he'd had enough
Of soothing words so kindly meant,
And helping hands so kindly lent.
He said, 'I've got one bone to pick:
These traffic wardens made me sick.
For years I've tried, God knows I've tried ...'
And with those words the poor chap died –
Brave-hearted warrior to the end,
And never short of ears to bend.

Underachievement

I'm a fan of Mountbatten of Burma,
But I wish I'd been Paddy Leigh Fermor.
I'm a handy old sod
If I'm given the nod,
But I'm stuck here in dull *terra firma*.

The Lead in the Boxing Glove

In Chipping Forelock, Oxfordshire,
The biggest cheese was Jimbo Spurr.
A parish councillor for years,
He held his own among his peers.
A small man (like his hero Proust) –
His dear wife Margie ran the roost;
But in the village he stood tall,
Like Caesar when he'd conquered Gaul.

But all too often Fate will shove
The lead into the boxing glove,
And great men will come crashing down,
Like Pagliaccio – poor clown.

One night, while in the Land of Nod,
The phone went. Jimbo said, 'Dear God!
Who can that be at half-past two?
Hello? Who's that? You what? To who?
I've never heard of such a thing!
Electric dungeon? Penis ring?
You must be mad. Oh, here's my wife.
I think *you* need to get a life.'

Now Margie was no silly prude,
But what she heard was, frankly, rude.
'Disgusting!' was her brisk retort.
'Good night,' she added with a snort.

Next night the same man rang again,
And several more in search of pain.
Night after night the calls poured in;
The Spurrs just took them on the chin.
But lack of sleep can take its toll
And Margie lost her self-control.
She said, 'If you don't sort this out,
I swear I'm going walkabout!'

Then Jimbo had a bright idea:
'It's not because they want *you*, dear.
Let's face it, it's not quite your bag.
An advert in a porno mag
Has used our number by mistake,
And hence your current bellyache.
I'm popping out. I shan't be long.
I'll see if I can right this wrong.'

He hurried to the village shop,
Where, like an undercover cop,
He scanned the shelves of magazines –
The *Vogues*, the *Harper's*, and the *Queens*.
His eyes looked up and there above
Were all the boobs and bums men love.

He looked around, the place was clear;
The owner, George, was nowhere near.
He stretched an arm, he seized *Big Tits*
And held it in his trembling mitts.
He opened up and riffled through;
His eyes popped out, his brain thought, Phew!

A voice said, 'Can I help you, sir?'
What followed next was all a blur.
George wore a silly, knowing grin,
And standing by a Mars bar bin
Was Trish, a local magistrate,
And one of Forelock's good and great.

Poor Jimbo's face had turned bright red.
The next thing was, he lost his head.
'This isn't what it might appear.
I'm looking for a number here.
It's not my fault. There's been a mess.
And someone's put the wrong address ...'

He gabbled on, and coughed and spluttered;
George nodded sagely, then he muttered,
'I understand, sir. Say no more.'
For Trish this was the final straw.
She shook her head and rolled her eyes;
Her feelings she could not disguise.

The last they heard of Jimbo Spurr,
He'd moved to north Carmarthenshire,
Where Margie runs a B&B,
And Jimbo makes the morning tea.
And no men ring at half-past two
To tell them what they'd like to do.

Nouveaux Pauvres

Susie and Nick are feeling sick –
The bank has rung warning bells.
Next year they may be forced to pick
Zermatt *or* the Seychelles.

Weekenders

When Don and James set off for Gwent
To weekend in the place they rent,
It takes an hour to pack the car.
The front step looks like a bazaar,
With Waitrose bags and crates of wine,
And tennis racquets, tied with twine,
A holdall full of windsurf gear,
Assorted plants, six-packs of beer,
Clean laundry from their previous stay,
And board games that they rarely play,
The dog's cage, biscuits, squeaky toys,
A pair of Don's old corduroys
To make the poor mutt feel at home,
Her bowl, her mat, her treats, her comb,
Her grooming brush, her cans and pouches –
They pack the lot, they are no slouches.
Compared with Pickfords at their best,
In packing terms, there's no contest.

From Holland Park to Ebbw Vale
(In Gwent) takes, via hill and dale,
Around three hours, give or take –
About right for a weekend break,
Depending on what time they leave.
To chance one's arm is plain naïve.
The boys are usually on their way
By eight a.m. on Saturday –
Though if their diaries are just right,
They'll get away on Friday night.

To watch them load their old hatchback
Is like that old-time circus act
When twenty clowns would fill a car
No bigger than a Kilner jar.

Beginning with the food and booze,
Enough to last a ten-day cruise,
They fill up every nook and cranny,
Their spatial skills are quite uncanny.
And on the back seat, to the right,
Behind the driver, out of sight,
There's room for one small cashmere rug –
The perfect spot for one small pug.

Bambina's their beloved's name;
It's seven years since madam came
Into their lives – their would-be child,
A loving daughter, sweet and mild.
There's nothing those two wouldn't do
To please their little Bubsy-Boo.

One Friday evening, South Wales-bound,
Near Wootton Bassett, Don turned round
To have a word with little Boo –
'Hello, there, sweetheart. How are you?'

He leant across, gave her a pat;
The rug was there, but that was that.

'Bambina, darling? Bloody hell …!
Where is she?' He'd begun to yell.

'You're joking!' James let out a groan.
The pair were both completely thrown.
He parked the car; they both got out;
He peered inside; there was no doubt.
Of Bubsy there was not a sign.
An icy chill ran down his spine.

The accusations ebbed and flowed
Across the middle of the road.
Both thought the other was to blame,
But it was just a pointless game.
The fact remained that they were there
And Bubsy-Boo was quite elsewhere.

They called each other twerps and prats,
And screeched like two Kilkenny cats
The whole way down the motorway,
With frequent breaks to groan and pray.

They came at last to Holland Park,
And on the pavement in the dark
Sat Bubsy-Boo, cucumber cool.
Unlike those two, she was no fool.

With shrieks of joy and boo-hoo-hoo,
They fell upon their Bubsy-Boo,
Who viewed them both with deep disdain,
Like Eleanor of Aquitaine
When, bored with Louis, King of France,
She booted him and took a chance
On Henry, Duke of Normandy,
Of far superior pedigree.

The humbler the pie they ate,
The less did she appreciate
Their treats, their toys, their coos, their hugs –
The little things that humour pugs.

If dogs could turn their noses up,
She would have won a silver cup.

They never went to Wales again;
The very thought caused too much pain.
Their partnership began to crack;
One day Don dealt his friend a smack.
Confused, Boo gave a high-pitched cry,
And sank her teeth into his thigh.

So, after that, she had to go –
To friends who lived in Pimlico,
And had a seaside house in Kent
Which Bubsy loved much more than Gwent.

And James and Don are now divorced.
It's no one's fault; they were not forced.
But, face it, no home's quite so sweet
Without a dog around your feet.

Caught on Camera

Achilles de Gray's a big cheese in PR,
Who enjoys all life's bounteous rewards.
He's a bit of a love-rat, as some types are,
And each year takes a large box at Lord's.

He invites lots of people he doesn't know well:
Mainly clients in showbiz and stuff,
And a chap called Roberto – a maître d'hotel –
And his boyfriend, a nice bit of rough.

He prefers it if everyone sits in full view
Of the spies in the Media Centre,
Where they may well be spotted by who-knows-who,
And picked out by a TV presenter.

He sits there himself, well exposed, in the middle,
One hand round a glass of champagne,
Getting up only when in dire need of a widdle,
Or to speak to his secretary, Jane.

One day he returned, feeling duly revived,
And a ghastly pain shot through his arse.
He leapt to his feet and found he'd contrived
To sit slap on his own champagne glass.

He yelled and he swore like the old Minotaur
As he tried to assess the damage.
He wasn't concerned with the pain: it was more
To do with his undercarriage.

And as Jane rubbed his bum with a soothing palm,
And smothered his face with kisses,
And cuddled him tight with a loving arm,
It was clear she could show him what bliss is ...

He twisted and turned and wriggled his hips
Like a Bollywood dancer in Delhi,
As his wife watched it all with well-pursed lips
On the screen of their drawing-room telly.

The Woman Who Found Her Arms Were Too Short

A bugbear for Amanda Mears
Was driving cars with manual gears.
At twenty she would lurch and hop,
Surprised to find herself in top.
She'd try to force the damned thing in
And make the most appalling din.
Her husband, Matt, would sigh and moan,
Like Mistrals blowing down the Rhone.
'For God's sake, woman, sort them out;
They're all in the same box,' he'd shout.

The day she bought an automatic
Her driving was far less erratic,
And thoughts of imminent divorce
Were soon replaced by true remorse.

Amanda, growing quite blasé,
Once popped to Brighton for the day
With Milly from next door but one,
And Maggot, who was rather fun.
The sun was shining as she wove
Her way along the coast to Hove,
And turned into a multi-storey,
Feeling pretty hunky-dory –
Until she reached the ticket thing
And found that she was struggling
To stretch her right arm out that far –
At least while sitting in the car.

'Oh dear,' she said, 'I never thought
My arms were really quite so short.
Don't move, you two; you stay right here.'

Forgetting she was still in gear,
She swung the door and stepped outside
And seized the ticket, arms spread wide,
In time to see the car proceed
At what one might call stately speed
Into the barrier and beyond,
Quite like a swan upon a pond.

It struck a Porsche and then a Merc,
And after that it got to work
On several brand new motorbikes,
A Golf, an Audi and the likes,
And came to rest against a wall –
As if after a road-rage brawl.

The damage stood at fifty thou,
And no one could explain just how
A clever woman without peer
Could not quite get her brain in gear.

Hallelujah

Ptolemy Smith has a lovely voice
(A lightish baritone by choice),
And recently he gave his all
With thousands at the Albert Hall,
Who pack it for the Scratch *Messiah* –
A massively ebullient choir.

His host, a breezy golfing chum,
Was very keen that he should come –
'For us it's just a bit of fun;
A good old sing-song, no harm done!
There's no rehearsal, no run-through,
And, frankly, we don't have a clue!'

But Ptolemy was no cheap slouch,
As friends and family will vouch.
He treats things like this seriously,
Declaring quite imperiously,
'One cannot take old Handel lightly;
He's thought to be the best – and rightly.'

So, every night for weeks ahead,
He mugged up on the score in bed,
Until he knew it off by heart –
At least, the baritone's main part.

But on the day a croaky throat
Produced the odd high croaky note,
So on the way he stopped and bought
A miniature of top class port
(A well-known recipe for pros,
As once prescribed by Berlioz),
And, pausing at the entrance door,
He took a swig and then some more ...

The wine began to warm and soothe;
His tonsils turned from rough to smooth,
And, like a carefree meadowlark
Ascending in a glorious arc,
His spirit soared, his voice burst free;
He warbled loud enough for three.

His jokey pals were most impressed
By Ptolemy's unbounded zest –
Though less so at the very end
When seven thousand loud 'Amen'-ed,
And, as the silence filled the hall
Before the last 'Amen' of all,
One voice rang out – a baritone
'Amen'-ing proudly on its own.

The golfers thought it quite a joke
And said, 'You *really* went for broke!
Why, anyone out there would think
That someone was the worse for drink!'

His friends now call him Pavarotti;
The poor chap's nearly going potty.

Georgina,
the Socialite Who Went to Pot

Georgina was a party girl;
Her life was one long social whirl.
At smart occasions every week
She'd meet the most exclusive clique
Of well-known names and lords and earls,
Good-looking men and pretty girls,
Assorted entries in *Who's Who* –
All generally well-to-do.

So dinner parties held no fears,
Not after thirty-seven years.
Polite, amusing and well-dressed,
She was the perfect party guest.
But then one day she lost her head,
And, frankly, wished that she was dead.

Pre-dinner with her best friend, Sybil,
A most delicious type of nibble
Stood near her in a flowery pot –
She very nearly ate the lot,
Until a fellow from Missouri
Said, 'Glad to see you like pot-pourri!'

The story spread, as did her fame
As Mrs Nutter – such a shame.
These days, when asked, she's never free –
A nervous social escapee;
And sits at home now, if you please,
With TV dinners on her knees.

The Golfer Who Was His Own Worst Opponent

Bob Kippax, it was widely known,
Preferred to play golf on his own.
He never, ever got depressed
Or, if he fluffed a short putt, stressed.
The great thing was, he'd always win.
No matter where they placed the pin,
Or what he scored by way of strokes,
He'd got the edge on other blokes.
And, what's more, liked to tell them so,
Propping the bar up, blow by blow.

His empty boasts began to grate,
And nasty rumours percolate –
Not least around the locker room
(And on the terrace, we presume),
That Bob was not what he appeared,
And well below the salt, one feared.

So, rather than incur a snub
And sharp expulsion from the club,
He took to playing after hours
When no one could deny his powers.

One evening, coming down the last,
When everywhere was overcast,
His second landed on the green –
The sweetest shot he'd ever seen.
A birdie followed, just like that,
And Bob, relieved, removed his hat,
And bowed to all the members, who
Had come outside to catch a view
Of one whose gifts they dared deny,
But now for which they'd surely die.

He bowed again, and waved, and beamed;
The lights behind the French doors gleamed.
He threw his fans a final glance ...
Then realised they were potted plants.

Up in the bar men shook their heads
As Bob slunk through the flowerbeds.
In golf clubs one's allowed to fail,
But lunacy's beyond the pale.

Now Bob plays at a pitch 'n' putt.
The club house is a wooden hut.
And no one cheers a hole in one
Where everyone is there for fun.

Drama Class

One thing we theatre-goers dread
Is finding that our neighbour's dead.
It seriously spoils one's evening so,
And makes one less inclined to go.

Giles Porringer, his ex-wife Jan,
Her sister and another man
Were sitting through a play by Shaw
When someone close began to snore.

The fellow in the seat in front
(For it was he) gave out a grunt.
His head went back, his jaw was slack –
The victim of a cardiac.

Some audience members sitting near
Began to shush and cough and peer.
The noise got worse, a nasty rattle
Like sabres in a Crimea battle
Now issued from his open maw.
Poor Giles thought, Cripes! He's dead for sure.

The man next door said, 'Hold my coat,
And push two fingers down his throat,
And grab his tongue. Don't let him choke.
One false move on your part, he'll croak.'

'Are you quite certain?' Giles hissed.
'I am a trained chiropodist,'
The man replied. 'A lucky chance.
I'm off to find an ambulance.'

And now a chilly silence falls
Across the stage, across the stalls,
As all the theatre longs to know
Which way this tragedy will go.

The lights go up and Giles is seen –
A most reluctant drama queen.

Two paramedics hurry through
With stretcher ready, right on cue.
They kneel down beside the stiff ...

Who clears his throat and gives a sniff,
And wakes out of a well-earned snooze
To find a total stranger who's
Got both his fingers down his gob,
While goggling like a halfwit knob.

'I've had enough of this!' he cried.
'Remove your hand and have some pride.
What is the theatre coming to?
It's worse than visiting the zoo.
It gives a decent chap the pip
Who cannot have an honest kip.'

Another moral for the list:
BEWARE ALL JOBS THAT END WITH -IST.

Cold Cuts

My in-laws came from Stourbridge
To see our brand-new house;
And all that I had in the fridge
Was cold, left-over grouse.

Déjà Vu in Oxford Street

Jack Huntsman had a rough divorce;
He thought his wife looked like a horse,
And told her so in unminced words,
And went off after younger birds.

While sauntering down Oxford Street
One day, a pair of dainty feet
Attracted his all-roving eye.
His heart leapt up, he gave a sigh –
Those shapely legs, that perky bum,
That swanlike neck, that shape, and some ...

He followed her to Bond Street Tube
While softly humming the 'Blue Danube'.
She paused. He stopped. He cleared his throat.
He buttoned up his cashmere coat.
He said, 'I'm not a Peeping Tom,
But when I see a real bomb—'

She turned. The smile froze on her lips.
His mouth dried up, as did his quips.

She said, 'You've got a bloody cheek.
My boyfriend told me that last week.
He means it, and I think, What luck,
But from my erstwhile husband – Yuk!'

Old School Ties

Mike is an old Fentonian –
A decent sort of guy.
He'd rather be Etonian,
And wear an OE tie.

But who knows where the dice will fall?
Or how life will pan out?
To be at public school at all
You're better in than out.

His school career was not the best;
His work was borderline.
He never wore a First Eight vest,
But still he made Top Swine.

Long gone the days of Toggers Room,
Back Passage and New Squits,
And Double Jankers (words of doom),
And washing in The Pits.

As Top Swine, he was hung about
With privilege galore.
At Refec he walked in and out
Through Tommy Tiddles' Door.

And, best of all, a Swine could stroll
On Pegram's Piece, no less,
And sit about on Arthur's Hole
And eat a Fenton Mess.

One day, Mike, O.F., 43,
Interior Decorator,
Decided on a whim to see
His dear old Alma Mater.

He picked a sunny Saturday,
And drove down via Chatham.
He parked his car near Mincers Way,
And strolled through Apthorpe's Bottom.

He breathed the healthy Kentish air;
He'd never felt so happy
Since shaving Halfshaft's pubic hair
While wearing a large nappy.

On Pegram's Piece a man called out,
'No strangers on the grass!'
Mike said, 'You're right, I have no doubt.
You may think me an arse.

'In fact I am not what I seem;
I am an old Top Swine –
An honour, one might say the cream,
In ninety sixty-nine.

'As such I have the perfect right
To walk on Pegram's Piece,
And, if I wish, to fly a kite,
And drive a flock of geese.

'Tradition is what made this school;
Tradition's what made me;
Tradition here has been the rule
Since eighteen ninety-three.'

'Now look,' said his inquisitor,
'You may have been a toff,
But now you're just a visitor,
So kindly bugger off!'

Mike's still an Old Fentonian.
But wears an OE tie,
And claims he's an Etonian,
And no one blinks an eye.

Sally-Anne, Who Mistook Herself for Mimi

The nation's keenest opera fan
Was Nico's cousin, Sally-Anne.
The Garden was her natural home;
Vienna, Paris, New York, Rome
Were other favourite stamping grounds
For wondrous sights and glorious sounds.
But, best of all, in summertime

There was no venue more sublime
Than Bogle Park in Gloucestershire,
Where opera's mounted *en plein air*.
She stayed with friends called Spencer-Gore,
Who owned the Rectory next door,
And after dinner every guest
Would stroll, immaculately dressed,
To where the most romantic tales
Competed with the nightingales.

One year the opera was *Bohème*;
The party list was much the same,
Except our heroine had a cough,
And would have called the whole thing off
(There's nothing like a few days' rest
When struggling with a nasty chest),
But couldn't bear to miss a note –
Or wear a nice warm overcoat …

The evening turned out grey and cold,
But on the stage it was pure gold.
The show went well, with great applause,
Then everybody trooped indoors,
Where Sally-Anne popped straight to bed,
And, by the morning, was brown bread.

With opera, the gravest sin
Is thinking you're your heroine.

Lowlights

For people who are colour blind
Life must prove quite a challenge.
Gus dyed his greying hair to find
He's prematurely orange.

Parent Power

Orlando was a journalist –
A good one, even slightly pissed.
He wrote on food, and wine, and sport;
His expertise was often sought
For pieces needed in a hurry
By glossy weeklies based in Surrey.
He rightly prided his renown
For never letting any down.

So when his perky daughter, Fay,
Accosted him one sunny day
To ask if he would help her write
An essay about Chaucer's Knight,
He didn't hesitate, or blink;
He made his mind up in a wink.
Though way outside his expertise,
He reckoned he could always squeeze
A few words out of anything,
From Heisenberg to Wagner's *Ring*.
You don't need to be academic;
A writer's talent is endemic.

'Leave it to me!' He tapped his nose,
And wrote a page of peerless prose –
Professional, well wrought enough
To stand alongside his best stuff.
Fay changed the odd word here and there
To give it a more youthful air,
And sweetly pecked him on the cheek,
And took it into school that week ...

When children's brains begin to slump,
It's all hands to the homework pump.
A quick leg-up is all they need
To help them get back up to speed.
Their gratitude is plain to see –
Though not when Dad gets them a D.

A La Recherche du Feather Boa

Sir Edward Tooley was the sort
Whose marriages were somewhat fraught.
At twenty-three he'd married Rayne,
But met a woman on a train,
Who'd given him a knowing glance
And whisked him to the South of France.

He married her, became a pa
And lived in St-Jean-Cap-Ferrat
For several years until he fell
In love with the exotic Belle –
A dancer at the Crazy Horse,
Who showed him lots of tricks, of course,
Including one with feather boas –
A practice known to real goers
Who swing this way (and sometimes that),
And often do it in a hat.

A marriage of full-on delight
Concluded when she saw the light
With Mrs Pike, became her slave,
And changed her name from Belle to Dave.

Now Ted was a quixotic bloke,
But this behaviour made him choke.
He felt there must be better ways
Of spending his maturer days
Than wasting time with women, who
Quite clearly hadn't got a clue
That underneath that waggish head
There lay a sober, serious Ted.

He wondered if he ever would
Meet someone who was kind and good.

But then at last he settled down
With dumpy, frumpy Margaret Brown,
A tour guide with the National Trust,
And owner of a queen-size bust,
Who, in her battered panama,
Looked oddly like his dear mama.

They lived for many years in Kent,
In Tenterden, in deep content.
With horses and assorted pets,
Adopted from the local vet's,
Among them Jack, the Border terrier;
As Margaret said, 'The more the merrier.'

Sir Edward joined the local choir,
Raised money for the old church spire,
And organised the village fete,
And holidayed in Bassenthwaite –
A figure in the neighbourhood,
A paragon of all that's good.

Dear Margaret was the perfect wife;
She guaranteed the perfect life.
She pandered to his every whim,
And never, ever bothered him.

And yet, for all her gentle ways,
He thought back to the good old days
Of sexy Belle and Cap-Ferrat,
Of wine and song and brouhaha,
And midnight swims with real goers,
And fun and games and feather boas.

The more his wife began to waddle,
The more he thought, A younger model
Is what a man of sixty needs –
And long blonde hair, and rings, and beads.

'I'm leaving you,' he told poor Meg.
'You'll think I am a rotten egg,
But really it is for the best.
There, now I've got that off my chest.'

She looked at him with pitying eyes.
'I think you're being very wise.
I'm leaving too and, furthermore,
The man I love is thirty-four.

'He's not the slightest bit like you;
He's got a funny mother, who
I'm told is quite a racy type
Who wears men's clothes and smokes a pipe.

'She's quite old now and lives in France.
I gather she once used to dance,
And mixed with what you might call goers,
And did strange things with feather boas.'

Now Edward lives with scruffy Jack,
Whose hair is thinning down his back;
But never mind, he's young at heart,
And, as dogs go, he's pretty smart.
The pair have moved to old Genoa,
Where people say Jack's quite a goer.

Back Story

Horatio's mother was no sage,
But on the subject of old age
Her talk was full of *bon*-ish *mots*,
And mental tappings on the nose.
'Don't bother to grow old, my dear;
There is no future there, I fear'
Was one she often liked to air,
Descending in her favourite chair
Amid the usual grunts ands groans
And puffs and pants and creaking bones.

Now Hozza's getting on himself,
And feeling slightly on the shelf,
Thanks largely to a painful back,
Which seems to baffle quack on quack.
And courses of manipulation,
Lashings of warm embrocation,
Swimming in the local lido
(Wearing quite a nasty Speedo) –
Nothing eased the non-stop tweak
Day on day and week on week.

A friend, Sid Eddis, had a wheeze:
Once in the Outer Hebrides
He'd skydived with a family friend –
'It's something I could recommend.
To free-fall through the air's one thing
With all the thrills that that can bring.
It's better than a superdrug.
But when you give the cord a tug,
It deals your system quite a jolt,
As if struck by a massive volt.
Now that might take your pain away
By stretching out your vertebrae.'

Horatio was a pragmatist
(And, not to say, empiricist).
His favourite maxim was 'Needs must',
To which he liked to add 'or bust'.
As treatments go, this seemed plain dotty,
But when a chap is going potty,
He'll clutch at any passing straw,
Or make for any open door –
Albeit at five thousand feet,
Connected to a man called Pete,
Who said, 'Just leave it all to me.
Relax, enjoy yourself, feel free
To wave your arms and scream and shout.
Up here there's no one else about.'

With that he launched them into space,
Like Victory over Samothrace.
Their arms spread wide, they plunged to earth,
And Hozza wondered, Is it worth
This trouble for a dodgy back?
And at that very moment – thwack!
The chute flew out. 'Geronimo!'
He shouted. 'Crikey! Here we go!'

The pain had flown. Like thistledown,
They floated oh so gently down,
And landed like two butterflies.
He couldn't quite believe his eyes
That he was safe back home again,
And, what's more, free at last from pain.

His parachute lay on the ground;
His friends and family gathered round.
He said, 'I've never felt so good
In all my life since childhood!'
He turned to give a hug to Pete;
His chute strings tangled round his feet;
He stumbled, took a backward trip,
Fell on his side and broke his hip.

When doing something new, do try,
To walk before you learn to fly.

Gastroshambles

Miranda is a brilliant cook,
But never does things by the book.
She improvises in a trice;
She'll chop and dice and chuck in spice,
And never gets caught on the hop,
Or dishes up a total flop.

But Lady Luck can be so cruel
And turn a great dish into gruel,
As happened just the other day,
When Ben's best friend, Sam, came to play.

'I'll give them supper,' she agreed.
There really wasn't any need
To go to town for two small boys,
Whose tastes for electronic toys,
Outweighed those for gastronomy
At supper, breakfast, lunch and tea.

She found some frozen mince. Of course!
Some meatballs in a pesto sauce
Should satisfy their inner men
And make sure Sam stays friends with Ben,

She fried them in a tick – hey presto!
And then disaster struck: no pesto!

She quickly made a sauce with cheese –
A standby that would surely please –
But felt she really must explain,
If only to assuage her pain.

Young Sam's face fell; he looked quite glum.
'No pesto!' he exclaimed. 'My mum
Puts pesto into everything.
Oh, dear; that's quite embarrassing.'

He ate the balls, but left the sauce:
It should have been Gruyère. Of course.

Now Ben's best friend's a boy called Pips,
Whose favourite food is egg and chips.
He eats Miranda's food and smiles,
And thinks she's the best cook by miles.

Putting on the Ritz

Young Harry is a journalist –
A travel-writing specialist.
While all his friends have full-time jobs,
He's satisfied with bits and bobs.
The freelance lifestyle suits him best;
Unlike his pals, he's never stressed.
With itchy feet, devoid of strings,
He loves the freedom travel brings.

And, more than that, he loves the fact
That others are so hugely hacked
That, unlike them, without a care,
He lives just like a millionaire
At other people's kind expense
For, frankly, little recompense,
Beyond a glowing piece or two,
Directed at the well-to-do.

He often travels in first class,
And treats his well-dressed, well-fed arse
To five-star luxury and more,
And mingles with the topmost drawer
From St Tropez to Angkor Wat,
And Necker Island on a yacht.
He acts the *crème*-ist *de la crème*
So well, they think he's one of them,
And drops names with a careless ease
Like garments in a cheap striptease.

Once, staying with fiancée, Sue,
He showed off to her parents, too –
The Hendersons in Potters Bar,
Who never ventured very far,
Or found themselves in hotels where
The customers routinely dare
To pilfer everything in sight,
Assuming that it is their right.

But Harry, anxious to impress,
With talk of every good address,
Held forth at lunch with travellers' tales
From Rajasthan to New South Wales,
Oblivious to their stifled yawns
Over the Marie Rose-dressed prawns.

That evening, as they met for drinks,
His hostess said amid the chinks,
'I do hope you don't mind, but I
Went in your room to cast an eye
And check that you've got everything –
A towel, some soap, that kind of thing.
But I see you've come well supplied.'

At that young Harry nearly died.
He'd unpacked earlier in haste,
And not the slightest bit shamefaced.
The contents of his Antler bag
Were scattered round, with all the swag
He'd nicked from myriad posh hotels,
Hand towels and unguents, shower gels,
An ashtray, slippers, flannel mitts,
A fluffy bathrobe from the Ritz …
With all their famous names displayed,
And every one of them top grade.

Though nothing more was said, it's true,
By Mrs H, he knew they knew.

The Frame Alone ...

The sharpest connoisseurs in town
Were Bill and Barbara Muspratt-Brown.
They specialised in British art;
They were not rich, but they were smart.
Habitués at private views,
They were the first to hear the news
Of who was buying what and where,
From Tring to Weston-super-Mare.
Both Friends of the Academy,
They were the pure epitome
Of art historians *manqués*,
Who know their stuff and what to say,
And fill their walls with frightful tosh –
Quite nice, but basically eyewash.

Babs dreamed of finding something great –
A painting worthy of the Tate,
Which would enhance their social stature,
And be a pension for the future –
One they could pick up for a song.
As experts, they could not go wrong.

'Fat chance,' said Bill. 'And pigs might fly,'
And added words like 'pie' and 'sky'.

But Fate is always lurking near
To catch you one behind the ear,
And Bill was well and truly floored
When, seated at his clavichord,
Babs marched in looking pleased as Punch,
At half-past twelve, in time for lunch,
Clutching a large plastic bag,
Just like a burglar with his swag.
'I've dreamed of something valuable,
And bought a little Constable
For twenty quid, not bad at all.
I found it on a market stall,'
She said. Bill, like a halibut, just goggled;
His pulse rate soared, his brain fair boggled.
She took it out. He said, 'By gum,
I think you've hit the jackpot, chum!
A *Study of the River Stour*!
In my view we could well insure
It for a hundred thou, at least.
In art I am no *arriviste*.
I know a Constable when I see one,
And I've no doubt that this could be one.
There's only one way to find out –
Give a top auction room a shout.
They'll want to see it straight away.
Get onto one without delay!'

The nice Bond Street receptionist
Was clearly not a specialist.
'I'll get someone to have a look.'
She took it to a little nook
Behind the desk and made a call –
'Could you, please, come down to the hall?
A lady has a Constable;
She thinks it might be valuable.'

A nice young man in pinstripe suit,
Who oozed good manners and repute,
Appeared and said, 'What have we here?
An English scene, it would appear.
A *Study of the River Stour.*
It's very neatly done, I'm sure.
But could it be the real McCoy?
Is this a lost piece by our boy?'

He hummed and hahed and coughed and sniffed,
Like one presented with a gift
Of two small eggs by Fabergé,
Who doesn't know quite what to say.

'I must admit,' he said at last,
'I've seen some copies in the past,
And to be frank, as copies go,
In my opinion this rates low.
With luck it might make fifty quid –
I doubt, though, if you'd get a bid.'

Now Barbara has a steady head,
But anybody would see red
Whose future life goes up in smoke,
Courtesy of some snooty bloke.

Poor Babs was absolutely thrown –
'*Just fifty?* But the frame alone …!'

The suit said, 'Let's not be verbose;
For me it verges on the gross.'

Still through the building came this moan –
'The frame alone …! The frame alone …!'

And now it hangs there on their wall,
And Babs reveals to one and all:
'Our little sketch by Constable.
Yes, I would say it's valuable.'

Bullitt

Now Roddy never went as far
As owning an exotic car.
The sportiest job he ever drove
(A clapped-out Triumph, painted mauve)
Was not the type to turn girls' heads,
Or get them jumping into beds.
A failed Clarkson through and through,
He raced a friend to Timbuktu,
But broke down in torrential rain
Outside a bar in northern Spain.

But still at heart a petrol-head,
His first move as a newly-wed
Was taking Liz to Silverstone –
The dullest day she'd ever known.

When he became a family man,
He bought a boring camper van –
An old converted Vivaro.
'A little dull, but it can go,'
He told his muckers in the pub.
He didn't want to risk a snub.

One day, while driving back from Slough,
He had the chance to show just how.
A Panda came up close behind,
And Roddy, thinking to be kind
And pull in so the chaps could pass,
Accelerated, like an arse,
To find the inside lane was full,
Like rush hour in Old Istanbul.

He couldn't find the tiniest gap
And got into a frightful flap
As on and on and on he flew,
Tailgated by the boys in blue,
Until his scramble for a place
Had turned into a full car chase.

They pulled him in near Baron's Court.
'I hate to be a spoilsport,'
Said one, 'You may be Stirling Moss,
But, frankly, I don't give a toss.
My name is PC Benedict,
And you are well and truly nicked.'

These days Rod rides a Boris bike
And, being ever sportsmanlike,
On early mornings, in the dark,
On pavements, crossings, in the park,
He'll never try to use his brake
If there's a chance to overtake.

Foot in Mouth Outbreak

Will Baskerville is twenty-eight
And rising through the ranks:
The sort of would-be heavyweight
Who flourishes in banks.

His pretty wife, called Anne-Marie,
Is also doing well.
She sells exotic pot-pourri
To well-heeled clientele.

The office party is the time
When young men like to shine,
And chaps like Will, who hope to climb,
Go easy on the wine.

So when his boss stepped in the lift
With wife in evening dress,
This had to be the perfect gift
For William to impress.

Now Tim, his boss, is fifty-four,
But those who meet him say
He could be thirty-five, no more –
A modern Dorian Gray.

His wife's the same age, give or take,
And looks exactly that:
A feisty woman, no mistake –
Quite small and slightly fat.

'My wife Penelope,' said Tim.
'This is our young star, Phil.'
Will shook her hand, and smiled at him.
'Some people call me Will.'

He waved a paw at Anne-Marie,
'And this is *my* mother,' he said.
He goggled at the other three
And promptly turned bright red.

His boss said, 'Nice to meet you, mum.
You're looking very well –
Unlike your son who's been struck dumb.
So … hail and farewell!'

There are certain situations
When you're fairly bang to rights.
Accept humiliations;
Save your strength for other fights.

A Word in Your Shell-Like

Men with the wrong shoes
May not be welcomed into
Polite society.

Red Trousers in Regatta Shock

Ned's trousers were red corduroy;
He wore a silk cravat;
One step above the hoi-polloi –
An ocean-going prat.
He sometimes sported purple trews,
And claimed to be a Scot.
His matching face was bright with booze,
His chit-chat utter rot.

A serious weekender,
He'd join the piss-head bunch –
A practised elbow-bender,
Well rat-arsed before lunch.

And, being quite oblivious
To those not in his set,
His conduct could prove bilious
To others that he met.

His voice was loud and booming;
It had a nasal drawl.
His presence, large and looming,
Was guaranteed to pall.

As for his ghastly bright red cords
(Unheeded by his chums),
They'd win the National Twat Awards
On far less outsize bums.

One day he met his Waterloo
At Henley, of all places,
When all the usual drinking crew
Rolled up with purple faces.

The oarsmen strained and bent their backs;
The men in pink caps roared;
But for these dipsomaniacs
The racing was ignored.

They lowered pint on pint of Pimm's,
Scoffed lobster, quaffed champagne,
And chanted silly made-up hymns;
Their jokes got more inane.

They partied on, the sky turned black
And, not to be outdone,
Some local rowdies in a pack
Turned up to spoil their fun.

It wasn't all Ned's fault, as such;
When nature called, he went.
He really couldn't see that much
Behind the nearby tent.

The Asbo, halfway through his smoke
Was feeling pretty rotten,
When suddenly this hooray bloke
Peed on his track-suit bottom.

Ned might have got away with it
By lobbing him some dough,
But, ever the red-trousered twit,
He told him where to go.

The two best sights that year, beside
The Maggie's Discotheque,
Was some man floating on the tide,
His red cords round his neck.

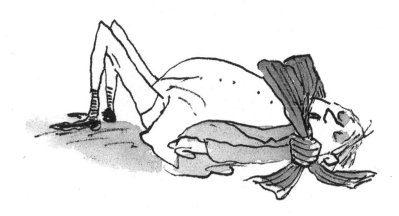

Dog Treats: An Assortment of Mutts, Mongrels, Puppies and Pooches

Introduction

'I can't think how anyone can live without a dog' is a phrase that is often to be heard on the lips of my dear wife and the mother of my children – a woman whom I would not be able to describe in such terms had I not been a dog-lover myself.

Kerry Blue terriers are our dog of choice and have been for the past thirty-five years. There was one in residence when I first met my wife in the early seventies. She was called Kerrels (the terrier, that is) and, as one brought up with dachshunds, it took me a while to establish a working relationship with an animal that was a good deal larger, hairier and more boisterous than anything I had been used to.

Kerrels's attitude to me was no less cool and for some time her gaze was (to quote P. G. Wodehouse on the subject of a similarly hairy dog in a Blandings novel) 'cold, wary and suspicious, like that of a stockbroker who thinks someone is going to play the confidence trick on him'.

Happily we developed a warm relationship and Kerrels became a central figure in both our lives.

Her successors have proved to be similarly whole-hearted members of the Matthew family: Milly, who used to come sailing with me and was the most easy-going crew I ever had; Hal, who had an over-developed sense of responsibility which he was never quite up to fulfilling; and, for the last eight years, Tippy, who in another life would have made a very good chairman of the local neighbourhood watch.

A friend once remarked of Kerrels that he thought she was really a human being wearing a dog outfit. I am not one to anthropomorphise animals, but I have counted all our dogs as close and much loved friends.

It is for this reason that many of the poems in this book are written from the dogs' point of view. I may have invested some of my subjects with thoughts and motives of which no animal could possibly be capable, but when you have experienced the very real feelings that a dog has for its owner, the sheer strength of will that many possess, and the huge range of human characteristics that all breeds display, you can't help thinking that there is a lot more going on in those furry heads than scientists would have us believe.

Emily Dickinson went further. 'Dogs are better than humans,' she wrote, 'because they know but do not tell.'

When my wife let slip to her many dog-walking friends that I was planning to write a book of poems about dogs, their owners and the eccentricities of both, several of them had stories to contribute – some funny, some sad, some bizarre, all well worth adapting into a few lines of rhyming verse. They have my grateful thanks, even if I cannot guarantee that they will necessarily recognise themselves, or their dogs.

Many famous owners have had heart-warming things to say about their dogs, but none has expressed more lyrically the pleasure that they bring to our lives than Milan Kundera: 'Dogs are our link to paradise. To sit with a dog on a hillside on a glorious afternoon is to be back in Eden where doing nothing was not boring – it was peace.'

Groucho Marx put it another way: 'Outside of a dog, a book is man's best friend. Inside of a dog it's too dark to read.'

Puppy Love

When Dad comes home at half past six,
I'm on him like a shot;
With leaps and bounds and slurps and licks
I give him all I've got.

I couldn't love a human more;
That's why I treat him rotten;
Then carry on as heretofore,
Attending to my bottom.

A Dog's Dinner

Our terrier Ted's a gastronome –
A dog who's very much at home
Where gourmet food is de rigueur,
And butter's often known as *beurre*,
And lobster is the scrap of choice,
And travel is by green Rolls-Royce.
Young Ted's a superstar chez nous –
A canine classic through and through:
A sort of doggy A. A. Gill,
Without the bite. His biggest thrill
Is lying very, very low
While waiting for our guests to go,
And, just as soon as he is able,
Climbing on the dining table
And scoffing anything that's left
With speed and skill one might call deft.
And not just food, but booze as well,
From Beaujolais and Muscatel
To coffee (black) and herbal tea,
While smidgens of the ripest Brie
And little blobs of chocolate mousse
(Mixed here and there with raspberry juice)
Are lapped up with a long pink tongue –
In terrier's terms, the perfect bung.

One night, amid the farewell schmooze,
Ted overdid it with the booze.
He polished off a glass of port,
And, rather as an afterthought,
A long-abandoned single malt:
It really wasn't *all* his fault.

The full effects were all too clear
As Ted turned obviously queer,
Beginning with a carefree pee
Against the custom-built settee,
While looking maddeningly smug,
Then puking on a Persian rug,
And crashing through the kitchen door,
And falling senseless on the floor.

Of course, we kicked up quite a stink.
From then on, Ted was off the drink –
And off the table, as it goes,
Along with his all-questing nose.

On dinner party nights, off-stage,
Incarcerated in his cage,
He now eats simple, homespun grub –
The sort you might get in the pub:
A fillet steak or chopped-up gammon,
Some lightly poached organic salmon,
A bowl of Highland Spring (not fizzy),
A toy to chew and keep him busy.

A dog that wears a human face
Is happier when he knows his place.

A Rose by Any Other Name

Now you can't call a puppy dog Eric,
Or Alan, or Graham, or Bruce,
Or Robin, or Norman, or Derek,
And to do so is plainly obtuse.

But some owners are not to be daunted;
For them any name would sound sweet.
If their poodle was Balzac, they'd flaunt it;
There's no limit to some folks' conceit.

It's a brave man who calls his dog Jesus,
And a braver one still who owns God;
And we know that there's some wag who'd tease us,
If we dared to shout 'Sit, Ichabod!'

You may smirk when an owner yells 'Rover!'
And 'Buster!' and 'Rex!' risk a laugh,
But the words 'Put it down, Casanova!'
Could disable a small seismograph.

Yet my cousins were really offended
The weekend they came down to stay,
When we said we'd not quite comprehended
Why they'd called their Great Dane Cher Bébé.

As names go, it's plain idiotic,
As the poor mutt knows better than they.
He is plain-as-a-pikestaff psychotic,
And in all probability gay.

When the fool did a runner at midnight,
And they shouted his name for an hour,
He ignored them, as any bright kid might:
We had no other choice but to cower.

Now we may have to think relocation;
We are getting some very odd looks.
The fact is that sheer affectation
Is a habit that nobody brooks.

Hooray for Hollywood?

My owner is an actress,
A model and DJ,
A long-time benefactress
Of causes in LA.

An author and designer,
A business woman too,
An expert in fine china,
A lover of Grand Cru.

Looks-wise, she's a humdinger,
With smiles that make men glow;
In good light a dead ringer
For Marilyn Monroe.

Her daddy has got billions,
And so, it seems, has she,
Considering the zillions
She lavishes on me.

My outfits are from Paris,
My overcoat is mink,
One hat's a tweed by Harris,
The other's silk, and pink.

My dog bowl's by Versace,
My collar's trimmed with gold,
My life is sheer *vivace*,
And I'm barely two years old.

I'm known in *the* best night spots –
A habit that I feed.
I'm on and off the right yachts
On my platinum-plated lead.

Tucked under madam's armpit,
Past cameras and paps,
I tread the old red carpet
With Clooney and the chaps.

By way of home expansion
To the basket I've outgrown,
She's built a doggy mansion,
Exactly like her own.

It's got a tiny staircase,
Designed for quadrupeds,
And chandeliers and clothes space,
And Chewy Vuitton beds.

With top-class air conditioning,
And drapes from Istanbul,
It's ideal positioning
Beside the swimming pool.

All's perfect till it hits you
That life is far from fair.
She's gone and bought a Shih-tzu,
So now I have to share.

A Dog He Would A-Wooing Go

As dogs go, I'm a gentleman;
I treat the ladies well.
A largely sentimental man,
I always ring their bell.

I'm not as half as randy as
Some Springers that I know,
Like next door's Ozymandias,
Who's always on the go.

He thinks he's in *The Great Escape* –
The Steve McQueen of Springers;
He's often getting in a scrape,
Like all true canine swingers.

The *on dit* in West Wittering
Among dogs in the loop
Is his sex life is quite glittering:
He's rarely in the coop.

The slightest opportunity,
He's off for rumpy-pumpy;
He acts with brash impunity –
He's permanently humpy.

Mind you, I blame his owner;
Jeff's one of nature's fools.
He's off now in Pamplona,
Being trampled on by bulls.

Last summer Ozzy came to stay
When Jeff was out in Spain.
I thought, but didn't like to say,
Well, this'll be a pain . . .

He never put a front paw wrong
The whole time he was here,
And never caused a ding-dong,
Or tried to disappear.

We took him down to Somerset
To weekend with a chum –
The owner of a pint-sized pet
Whose name was Sugar Plum.

This Papillon, to her surprise,
Was at that time on heat;
Full marks, then, for the enterprise
Of local vet called Pete.

A quick jab in the derrière
Meant she was safe and sound,
And risked no sudden disrepair
From any passing hound.

Now I'm not one to be outdone
If offered half a chance
To try it on with anyone
Who asks me to the dance.

But when a girl protests to you,
'I'm sitting this one out,'
The best thing that a chap can do
Is take a walkabout.

But some dogs have no savoir-faire;
They'll always chance their arm.
They wouldn't think; they wouldn't care;
They've never heard of charm.

Our friends came out to say hello,
And, wiggling her bum,
Like some white doggy furbelow,
Was little Sugar Plum.

Next thing, a sight to make one quail –
A really weird depiction:
Two heads, six legs, a bouncing tail –
A beast from science fiction.

No prize for guessing what it was,
Or who was under who.
Beware the sex-mad dog, because
You don't know what he'll do.

Club Man

I'm what you'd call a club man;
I live off Piccadilly.
My dad was more a pub man,
Well known as Pale Ale Billy.

He was a huge attraction
Down at the Eel and Cockles –
A great weekend distraction
For countless crowds of grockles.

He'd stand there on his hind legs
Behind the public bar
Among the pumps and beer kegs
And crack into a jar.

But, sad to tell, drink took its toll;
Bill's life was diabolic.
He fell into a deep, dark hole –
A serious alcoholic.

He never lived to see his son
Achieve his great ambitions
To know a world of wealth and fun
In privileged positions.

But life is often hit and miss:
To cut a story short,
I moved to the metropolis,
And luckily was bought

By Malcolm, a true connoisseur,
A poet of repute,
An art collector, restaurateur,
And business man to boot.

The nicest kind of millionaire
(The nicest I have known),
He had a club in Berkeley Square.
The style was all his own:

Fine furniture, delicious food
To please the gastronome;
A calm and reassuring mood –
The perfect home from home.

And none was more relaxed than me;
I'd sit there in the hall.
I liked to keep a weather eye
On members one and all.

For owners who were well behaved
Their dogs were always welcome –
Though in my case all rules were waived,
As right-hand man to Malcolm.

I'd wander through the Whistler Bar,
And settle here and there,
Enjoy the taste of caviar,
And watch *chemin-de-fer*.

The club was my old stamping ground
For many, many years –
A thoroughly contented hound,
A star among my peers.

But then, like Lucifer, one day
I had a mighty fall.
This carefree boulevardier
Found an Afghan in the hall:

An ocean-going bossy boots;
A stuck-up bitch called Jess –
The kind that doesn't give two hoots:
My life was in a mess.

When women throw their weight about
In any smart gents' club,
The answer is to say, 'I'm out,'
And head off to the pub.

Which is why these days you'll find me
Propping up the public bar
In the Cockles, and behind me,
The ghost of dear Papa.

Dumb Friend

Old Einstein was a brainbox
Who well deserved his fame;
So how come Tom and Thane Cox
Gave their Newfoundland his name?

He can be very plucky,
With all that courage brings,
But when he's feeling yucky,
He does the weirdest things.

He licks the Wilton carpet
In all the oddest places,
And sometimes tries his armpit,
And once ate someone's braces.

He stands for ages staring
At a small hole near the door,
In case a mouse comes haring
Across the kitchen floor.

It never has, and never will;
We've told him he should chill it:
A builder made it with a drill
And then forgot to fill it.

He is a total idiot –
In human terms, a prat.
Not even T. S. Eliot
Had such a stupid cat.

There's no hint of intelligence,
As far as one can tell,
But plenty of intransigence –
Dim wittedness as well.

He'll hump an old sports jacket
If it's hanging on a chair,
And make a frightful racket,
Though there's no one anywhere.

Or eat a massive bowlful
Of biscuits and tinned meat,
Then stand there looking soulful,
Still gagging for a treat.

But is his brain so foggy?
Is that the way dogs tick?
Is he bog-standard doggy,
And I'm the one who's thick?

Labradoodle Dandy

I'm a lovely Labradoodle;
A Labradoodle do or die;
A perfect mixture of two handsome breeds –
A thoroughly regular guy.

I've got an owner who's a noodle –
An utter nitwit through and through.
Mr Noodle came to town,
A would-be Casanova;
He drives a Maserati and
The damned fool calls me Rover.

Walkies

My owner is a busy bee –
A big cheese in the City.
He doesn't have much time for me,
Or girlfriends, more's the pity.
He takes me out at crack of dawn
So I can have a widdle
And make light patches on the lawn:
His motives are a riddle.

He's not a cruel man per se,
Of that there is no doubting.
A walker turns up every day
And takes me on an outing.
And, yet, to own a lively mutt
And *never* take it walkies,
You have to be some kind of nut –
As soft as pastel chalk is.

I must admit, I'm quite a lad,
And lots of fun, to boot.

I sometimes go completely mad;
I can be quite a hoot.
I roll in every nasty smell
With Mac, my pal the Scottie;
And rush around and bark like hell,
Which drives the walker potty.

She's really quite a friendly soul;
Her name's Ekaterina.
She does a good job on the whole,
But could be a lot keener.
She's always on the telephone
In fluent Lithuanian;
She might as well be on her own,
Like Fritz, the Pomeranian.

She natters on for hours and hours
And wanders up and down,
And picks at various wild flowers,
And always wears a frown.

I'm not a dog that makes demands
Like others that I know,
Who turn deaf ears to all commands
Just when it's time to go.
And Spartacus, the Kerry Blue,
Goes stalking some poor squirrel;
And Claud, the little Cockerpoo,
A Labrador called Cyril,

And Zebedee, the Afghan hound,
All wander here and there,
And generally muck around
And, frankly, couldn't care.

It's water off a duck to me;
I never say a word,
Or ever seem to disagree,
Or give the swine the bird.

But yesterday I'd had enough
Of being messed about.
The time had come to play it tough,
And demonstrate some clout.

I'm really hacked at being bumped
By Albrecht, the Alsatian;
And even more at being humped
By Bert, the fat Dalmatian.

So when Miss Lithuania
Got busy on the blower
With motley miscellanea,
I slid off like a boa,
And legged it past the Serpentine,
Through flora and through fauna,
While gently humming 'Auld Lang Syne',
And crossed near Hyde Park Corner.

I could have gone straight home from there,
And put her mind at rest,
But, come along now, fair is fair:
Would *you* care if she's stressed?

I really don't get out that much,
I have no chance to roam;
I'm stuck for ever in the hutch,
So why should I go home?

I strolled around Belgravia,
A carefree little chap,
And met a pup called Xavier,
And had a little yap.

I had some lunch at half past two
Just down the road from Tesco –
A rather nasty Danish blue
(I gladly let the rest go).

I had a snooze, then met a bloke
Who tickled my left ear,
And gave me half a can of Coke,
And quite a lot of beer.

I thought, I really love the smell
Of freedom and release.
So what if I don't eat so well?
You can't beat inner peace.

So now I'm what they call a stray –
A freelance, if you like.
This dog can walk alone all day;
The rest can take a hike.

Gobbledogook

In dog terms, I'm not intellectual;
My word count is tragically low.
My cognitive power's ineffectual;
I'm as likely to 'wait' as to 'go'.

I can understand 'sit', 'have a widdle',
'Good boy', 'in your basket', 'get down',
But most words are an out-and-out riddle.
Can you wonder I act like a clown?

At the mention of squirrels or rabbits,
I am off as if shot from a gun.
You can tell I'm a creature of habits –
As a mate I am second to none.

I know when my owner is happy,
And it's only too clear when he's cross.
On the whole I'm a happy young chappie,
And I know all too well who's the boss.

But his habit of nattering floors me;
All I hear is a jumble of sounds.
I can't say it totally bores me,
But it practically always dumbfounds.

Is he trying to warn me of danger?
Feeling doleful about his ex-wife?
Has he spotted an odd-looking stranger?
Is he pondering the meaning of life?

Is he quoting from something on telly?
Or a poem he's learnt off by heart
By Larkin or Percy Bysshe Shelley?
Or *bons mots* by some pundit on art?

And what about all that charade stuff?
An impression perhaps? But of who?
As games go, it's seriously hard stuff;
If only he'd give me a clue.

They say that all dogs and their owners
Can communicate perfectly well.
I hate to be one of life's Jonahs,
But communicate? Can they hell!

First Dogs

We are the President's dogs. Hello.
My name is Sunny. His is Bo.
I think that's all you need to know.
So . . .
Nice to meet you. Cheerio.

Peke Condition

A lion loved a marmoset, or so the legend goes,
But found that he was much too big and suffered bitter
   woes.
He went to see the Buddha who said, 'Here's a nice
   surprise,'
And waved his hand and, magically, transformed the
   lion's size.

The pair then got together and before you could say
   'Please',
They had a fluffy offspring and they named him
   Pekingese.
The courage of a lion and the cunning of a monkey,
Together made a fearsome beast – a bruiser, if not
   hunky.

The emperors of China carried small ones in their
   sleeves,
And fed them curlew livers, breasts of quail and fresh
   goat's cheese.
The Empress Dowager Cixi (pronounced Tzu-hsi, as
   you know)
Compiled a list of qualities that Pekingese should
   show:

Among them bandy forelegs, tufted feet and coal black
    face,
Ears like war junks, eyes like saucers, silent footfall,
    knows its place.
In its manner entertaining, yet pure-driven like the
    snows,
And, if faced with foreign devils, trained to bite them
    on the nose ...

As witness statements go, this doesn't quite describe
    the incident;
You could say it was just another rather silly accident.
There's no good reason why Ping-pong attacked the
    Scotsman thus,
As we were standing innocently, waiting for a bus.

To shove your face in any dog's is asking for a nip,
And for some unknown reason this chap gave poor
    Ping the pip.
It could have been his tone of voice, his patronising
    air,
His silly face, his aftershave, his rather nasty hair.
Or was there something more to it? Was history on
    Ping's side?
Did Buddha whisper in his ear? Some supernatural
    guide?
The legends of the Orient are cloaked in age-old fog –
The Chinese are a mystery. So is the Lion Dog.

Pillow Talk

A Pinscher's not the ideal dog to have with you in bed;
Of all companions he's not what you'd call a sleepyhead.
He fidgets and he mumbles, he has bad breath and he
     snores;
Of all the men I've slept with, he would top my list of
     bores.
And that includes my husband, who in bed terms is a hog.
All things considered, I would really rather have the dog.

Show Dog

Like dear old Noel Coward, I've a talent to amuse,
And I'm very glad to say that it's a talent I can use.

My acting name is Johnny (though my family call me
    Buster);
I may not be a Gielgud, but it adds a certain lustre.

Our lot have been theatricals since 1964 –
An odd career for spaniels who are straight from the
    top drawer.

My great-great-grandpa was in rep (in Frinton, since
    you ask),
As Charles the Second's lapdog in a Restoration
    masque.

He spent some downtime 'resting' for a few months
    after that,
Then did a quick voice-over for a scene in *Postman Pat*.

He broke into commercials with an advert for baked
    beans:
There is no doubt about it, I've got greasepaint in my
    genes.

He nearly landed Chunky Meat with model Patti
    Boyd,
But lost out to that bloodhound and the gloomy
    Clement Freud.

We've had our ups and downs, of course, like all good
    actors do;
My father had a triumph with Chris Biggins at the zoo.

He could have been a big screen star and won Palm
    Dog awards,
But misbehaved with Stephen Fry while filming on the
    Broads.

The family had great hopes for me; my rise was
    meteoric;
At training school my parody of Lassie was historic.

But life for dogs on stage and screen is something of a
    lottery;
My first job was in evening classes, posing for some
    pottery.

So then I changed my agent and the jobs came thick
    and fast;
I got a nice commercial for a new Elastoplast.

I did some well-paid paw work for a TV show called
    BARK! –
A so-called comedy for kids with jokes straight from
    the ark.
My agent was an imbecile – he put me up for Toto;
The fool could see I'm not a Cairn by looking at my
    photo.

Then Uggie came and swept the board with well-
    trained terrier bustle,
And you could whistle for a job if you weren't a Jack
    Russell.

I sat around and nothing came: it almost drove me
    bats;
I was seriously thinking of auditioning for *Cats*.

And now the phone's gone silent, as I dream up things
    to do,
Like writing a synopsis for a book on canine poo.

But, still, I'm very happy in the actors' home for dogs,
And my fellow guests seem happy with my wistful
    monologues.

Oh Deer

George was going to call me Clinton –
Cracking name for a dog full of zest;
But bizarrely they changed it to Hinton:
Ever since, I have felt second best.

I have never fulfilled my potential;
I am never entirely on song.
I try to appear deferential,
But how can I when he's mostly wrong?

One wonders how ever they breed 'em;
They've less brains in their heads than a swede.
I am rarely allowed real freedom;
I spend most of my time on a lead.

There's no violence at all in my make-up;
A Dalmatian's a peaceable sort;
All it takes is a half-decent wake-up,
And I'm action-packed, ready for sport.

My epiphany hit me last Sunday
While strolling in Knole Park in Kent.
What started for George as a fun day
Ended up as a hellish lament.

I am not one for making excuses,
But some smells don't half get up your nose,
And release your most primeval juices,
And thus cause you to metamorphose.

Now, some deer are unusually fragrant,
And they make no attempt to disguise
Their disdain for us dogs, which is flagrant;
You can tell by the look in their eyes.

And, frankly, I couldn't resist it;
I slipped out of my collar and went.
No dog worth his salt would have missed it
For anything, given that scent.

I could hear George's voice way behind me,
Yelling 'Hinton!' again and again.
I knew he'd be lucky to find me;
He isn't the fastest of men.

'Oh, bloody hell, Hinton!' he bellowed.
'Why the hell don't you do as you're told?'
The leaves I had noticed had yellowed,
And the landscape was turning to gold.

Though around me the summer was dying,
I felt it was springtime again,
And at times I could swear I was flying
Like Nureyev with Margot Fonteyn.

But a dog is no match for wild creatures;
As some men came and took me away,
I remembered that saying of Nietzsche's:
'Life is rarely one long holiday.'

Next morning they came to collect me
After twelve hours locked in a shed.
I was worried that George would reject me,
But he hugged me and patted my head.

I did not take his kindliness lightly –
Licked his hand as he opened the door;
And I sat in the back seat politely,
And was violently sick on the floor.

War Dog

I was just a yellow Labrador Retriever;
As a puppy, I had fun and chewed old shoes.
I was not what you might call a great achiever,
Or the sort of dog that everyone might choose.

I was not a lot more boisterous than others,
Though I didn't always heed my owner's calls,
And I think I may have worried some young mothers:
I couldn't get enough of chasing balls.

That's all I did for weeks of so-called training,
And I learnt to sit and do as I was told.
Life with Sergeant Briggs was highly entertaining,
And, as mates go, he was seriously pure gold.

It surprised me when they gave me to the Army,
Though I never really felt I was a pet,
Or the kind of dog that drives a family barmy:
Playing games all day is really not a sweat.

I still have no idea why Briggsy picked me,
Or thought I had a nose for IEDs.
I liked balls, not roadside bombs – he might have tricked
      me:
I was just a simple mutt who loved to please.

I have never had a yearn for foreign places,
And I've never been a big fan of the heat.
So, plodding round in scorching, dusty spaces
Was not my idea of the perfect treat.

Camp Bastion was not what you'd call homely;
A claustrophobic cage is not a bed.
But, with other dogs around, you're never lonely –
Though I sometimes felt a little better bred.

To tell the truth, the work was easy-peasy;
I could smell an IED from miles away.
I'd just sit there looking, frankly, pretty cheesy,
Till he threw my ball, and then I'd get to play.

There had been, they said, the odd quite hairy moment,
Though bombs smell much the same to dogs like me.
I liked my work and knew what 'yes' and 'no' meant;
I was always pretty good as a trainee.

I don't know why I got the Dickin Medal –
What is sometimes called the animal VC.
The hero's life is not for dogs to peddle –
Not even if they're fêted on TV.

For life as a search dog is not all roses;
The Taliban could often catch you out.
And no matter what a miracle your nose is,
Chances were that they might have the final shout . . .

I am one of several hundred dogs who copped it,
And tripped a wire before they got the scent,
And pushed on when they really should have hopped it,
And, like the way of all dog flesh, they went.

So now I'm just a footnote in dog history –
A name carved on a small memorial stone.
For those who know my story there's no mystery
As to who comes by each week and leaves a bone.

Canis Latinicus

Quantum costum ille canis in fenestra (*arfus, arfus*),
Ille unus cum vibrato fundo?
Quantum costum ille canis in fenestra? (*arfus, arfus*)
Ego spero ille canis vendibilis est.

Necessarium est ire ad Californiam,
Et relinquere meum inamoratum solum.
Si habet canem non erit desolatus,
Et canis habebit bonum domicilium.

Non volo rabbitum aut felix.
Non volo psittacum qui loquit.
Non volo crateram pisciculorum –
Impossibilis cum pisce ambulare.

Quantum costum ille canis in fenestra (*woofus, woofus*),
Ille unus cum vibrato fundo?
Quantum costum ille canis in fenestra? (*woofus, woofus*)
Ego spero ille canis vendibilis est.

Jack the Nipper

Jack Sparrow was an anxious dog –
A worrier all day and night.
His life was one huge catalogue
Of tasks to tackle, wrongs to right.

His sense of duty weighed him down,
Like Atlas pressed beneath the globe.
In village street, or park, or town,
He was a classic sociophobe.

Now Jack was never more neurotic
Than bossing friends around his home:
His attitude was plain despotic,
And showed a curious chromosome.

While other dogs, like Cerberus,
Stood sentinel-style at the door,
Jack's welcome was as generous
As Guildenstern's in Elsinore.

But once guests dared to say farewell,
Or made the slightest move to go,
From that time on, their life was hell,
For, like an arrow from the bow

Of one who'd fought at Agincourt,
He'd catch them in the entrance hall,
And there enjoy his favourite sport
Of pinning them against the wall.

Nobody was allowed to leave –
Not even those who lived with him.
They had no choice but to deceive,
Or risk the feel of tooth on limb.

To save him grief (and save them pain),
They'd sneak out through the garden gate
And head off via the nearby lane,
And leave poor Jack to sit and wait.

It worked okay, this clever ploy,
Until, depressed by winter blues,
They called a cab, said, 'Stay! Good boy!'
And set off on a worldwide cruise.

While queuing at the check-in desk,
The wife began to shake and bawl,
'It can't be true! It's too grotesque!
We've left our passports in the hall!'

They got back home just after tea;
Jack wouldn't fall for that again.
Now they were truly all at sea,
Like sad sheep guarded in their pen.

One day they gave the beast away
Following *that* episode
(The postman's better, by the way)
To Ron and Vera up the road,
Who very rarely leave the house,
Thanks largely to senility.
And now Jack's quiet as a mouse,
Freed from responsibility.

Passing Thought of a Dog Lover

Those who do not smile
At dogs who walk by on leads
Do not have real souls.

A Friend in Need

Amanda was a happy girl;
She had a carefree life.
She married in a glorious whirl;
She was the perfect wife.

Her husband, a solicitor,
Was rich as he was handsome;
A natural competitor –
A *ne plus ultra*, and some.

No matter what she drank or ate,
She still stayed slim and supple.
In jeans or evening dress, no sweat,
They made the ideal couple.

Their baby, Tom, was *sans pareil* –
They put him down for Eton.
As lifestyles go, you'd have to say,
Theirs had to be unbeaten.

They bought a little Kerry Blue,
A perky chap called Paddy.
They walked on Saturdays in Kew –
Amanda, Tom and Daddy.

And then one day her husband, Nick,
Seduced his secretary.
Just looking at him made her sick,
And life was far from merry.

She moved into a little pad –
A single girl, and mother,
With Paddy and her little lad:
No room there for another.

The day she got divorced was hell;
She sat there feeling grotty;
And as the tears began to well,
She thought, 'I'm going potty.

'I'm done with men, I'm done with sex,
Deceit and cruel rejection.
I don't miss love, my home, my ex,
But, oh, I miss affection.'

Now, Paddy never got on chairs;
He thought, 'It is bad manners
For dogs to give themselves false airs.
Why else would owners ban us?'

But as the saying goes, needs must,
As dogs know all too well.
Next thing, he lands slap on her bust –
Her heart begins to swell.

He lays his head upon her knee,
Looks up with loving eyes.
For dogs, as any fool can see,
Are very, very wise.

Scientific Experiments on Dogs

I do think 'dog psychologists' can talk a load of twaddle;
They seem to think that recognising how we think's a
　　doddle.
Some say that just by looking you can tell how we are
　　feeling.
That theory is, I have to say, decidedly revealing
About the human intellect – not canine powers of
　　thought,
Which often can produce ideas of quite a different sort.

A German Shepherd that I know – the son of my best
　　buddy –
Agreed to be the subject of a scientific study.
He simply had to sit there while these people in white
　　coats
Did funny things to him and then took photos and made
　　notes.
They tried to make him happy, and disgusted, and
　　afraid,
With praise and nasty medicine and a furious tirade.
His ears pricked up and then went flat, he showed his
　　whites of eyes;
They burst a large balloon quite near to stimulate
　　surprise.

They published the results (with pics) in one of the posh
    papers,
And chronicled the details of their scientific capers.

But can one read emotion in a wrinkle on a head?
Can the angle of an ear reveal reaction to what's said?
A shepherd dog is smooth of face, its eyes are clear to see;
But have they tried a hairy Bearded Collie, just like me?

Dog Treats

I have tried every mixer and biscuit,
Tasty kibbles of turkey and rice;
And one day I thought I would risk it
With a fish-flavoured snack, which was nice.

I've enjoyed complete dry foods by Chappie,
Wellbeloved, Eukanuba and Spratt's,
But I'll tell you what makes me most happy –
That's the biscuits made specially for cats.

Arthur and Augustus

Arthur's Story:

I'm not a big dog lover, like some people that I know;
I can take take 'em, I can leave 'em – easy come and
    easy go.
So, imagine my surprise when, in the lounge, what
    should I see
But this great big hairy monster stretched out on my
    best settee.
I think he's a St Bernard: well, I ran a few quick checks –

You know the dogs I mean, with little barrels round
	their necks.
I don't know how he got there, it was not by
	invitation;
I guess it must have been a stroke of prestidigitation.
I thought he'd do a runner, but he lay there bold as
	brass,
So I hadn't got the heart to say, 'Oi, sunshine: off
	your arse.'
He stayed all afternoon, then after tea he gave a yawn,
Got up, went out the back and had a widdle on the
	lawn.
I let him out the front and off he toddled down the
	street –
As nice a dog as you and I could ever hope to meet.
But, blow me down, next morning he was standing at
	the door;
I let him in, he settled down and slept from ten till
	four.
He's been round every day since then and has a good
	long zizz.
He never wants to eat or drink; I don't know who he
	is.
He's one of life's great mysteries, like Santa or the Yeti.
Or why most space is black as ink. Or why I married
	Betty.
One day I may discover why on earth he's chosen me;
Meanwhile, I just accept that I have got a dog for free.

Augustus's Story:

I'm not a fussy animal, like some dogs that I know.
If someone says it's time for bed, then off to bed I go.
If I think I'm going walkies and I land up in the vet,
I never dig my heels in, or look miserable, or fret.
I turn deaf ears to fireworks and gunfights on TV –
That's not to say I like them, but they never bother me.
If people shower affection when I'm dozing in my
    basket,
I'm happy to accept it, though I'm not a dog to ask it.
In fact, one way and another, I'm an easy-going chap,
And, at twelve years old, I think that I'm entitled to a
    nap –
Which, frankly, isn't easy with small children in the
    house;
It's my bad luck my owner had to choose a younger
    spouse.

247

There's three of them – so far, at least – aged five, and
    three, and one,
And, speaking as an older dog, they're not enormous
    fun.
The five-year-old annoyed me when he walked off
    with my chews,
So I tasted sweet revenge by chewing up his favourite
    shoes.
The small one pulls my whiskers or my tail when I
    snore,
And the other tips my dinner in the middle of the
    floor.
I don't ask much from anyone, except a little kip,
But all I get is constant noise and pretty non-stop gyp.

I'm nothing if not cunning and I put my brain to
work,
And I couldn't help but notice that this neighbour,
who's a berk,
Leaves his front door open every time he goes to fill
his bin,
So I slipped round there one morning and the next
thing, I was in.
My owner's not too bothered, and I know it's frightful
cheek,
But at least I get my head down four or five times
every week.
I'd really like to live there, since the journey's quite a
flog:
Can one claim right of asylum – as a poor, hard-done-
by dog?

One

One has a pretty cushy life,
Comparatively free from strife,
In large-ish, comfortable digs –
You'd hardly say one lives like pigs.

One's town house has extensive grounds;
One barely hears the traffic sounds.
Wide lawns, a pond – that's all one needs;
One never needs to strap on leads
And go for 'walkies' in the park,
Or any of that urban lark.

One's owner has a Berkshire pile;
One weekends there in decent style.
One's summer hols are spent in heather,
Picknicking in dubious weather.

One loves the north, East Anglia too –
There's such a lot for one to do.
While others fish and shoot and ride,
One potters round, or stays inside.

As owners go, she's so enchanted
That every little wish is granted.
One dines on steak and chicken breast.
The gourmet chef serves up the best.

The chap who brings it in's ex-navy,
But she herself pours out the gravy.
One cannot start till she says 'Eat'.
Who cares when each meal's such a treat?
No titbits, mind, the regime's strict,
So every bowl is strictly licked.

When being fitted for a dress,
She saves us all from pain and stress,
And combs the floor for nasty pins,
And drops them into nearby bins,
And keeps small magnets in small drawers,
For fear of harming tender paws.

A long life and a merry one,
It's been a gas; a lot of fun:
A royal drama, ups and downs,
And ins and outs – send in the clowns.

A sort of canine Bess and Porgy –
Though in our case it's Bess and Corgi.

Lost in Distraction

Has anybody seen my dog?

I looked at my mobile for half a minute,
Just to check there was nothing in it.
And while I was scrolling, he got distracted.
I realise now, I should have acted ...
Has *anyone* seen my dog?

Excuse me, have you seen my dog?

He's only a puppy. An English red setter.
You really can't miss him, he's wearing a sweater.
It's green. Like a jacket. Because of the weather.
When I say green, it's more like heather.

He can't have gone far. Has he gone to the car?
Is there really a need for this brouhaha?
But there is the road –
And that poor squashed toad . . .

Please, *somebody* find my dog!

How was your Christmas?

The Alsatian came in like a wolf on the steppes
(Rex isn't a creature who tiptoes or schleps);
With his nose on the twitch and his prey in his sight,
His lips were well licked and his teeth were pearl
    white.

Mrs Unthank was out in the kitchen, as per,
While her husband – a self-styled wine connoisseur –
Was dispensing champagne in the lounge to the gang,
Both determined that Christmas would go with a
    bang.

Lunch was ready to serve as the hall clock struck two,
So she fluffed up her hair, washed her hands and came
    through.
'When you're ready,' she said, and she reached for a
    drink.
'Happy Christmas! And one of the best, I would
    think.'

The table for twelve was more perfectly laid
Than the best TV advert that's ever been made.
The Waterford glass shone like stars on the sea,
And the candlelight danced with the lights on the tree.

The sideboard was piled with traditional fare,
And the steam from the vegetables rose in the air,
And the skin of the turkey glowed golden and moist,
And they all raised their glasses, cried 'Cheers!' and
    rejoiced ...

Or they would have done, had the old turkey been
    there,
But it seemed that the bird had flown into thin air.
They stared wildly around like our lads at Rorke's
    Drift
When the Zulus got ready to give them short shrift.

'It was there just a moment ago,' shrieked the cook.
Her eyes were on stalks and her whole body shook;
And it shook even more when in through the door
Stepped young Rex with a turkey leg clamped in his
    jaw.

The mangled cadaver lay out in the hall;
The dog looked embarrassed, but that wasn't all.
He coughed and he swallowed and started to choke:
It was clear that a bone had got stuck in his throat ...

The vet bill amounted to several thou,
And their friends and their family all marvelled at how
The two Unthanks appeared to remain so assured,
When they found they'd forgotten to have Rex
    insured.

Foreign Body

I do not like that pert Maltese;
God knows, I'm not that hard to please.

I've put up with his funny ways,
His silly homosexual phase,
His look of absolute disdain
That time I holidayed in Spain.
We've all of us had highs and lows,
And sniffed strange odours up our nose,
And done our business on the pavement,
Yet known what being very brave meant.

But some dogs are like aliens –
To be precise, Australians –
The kind that sledge in Ashes Tests,
And flex their arms and beat their chests,
And try to make themselves sound tough,
And pose as some girl's bit of rough.

And when this ratbag had a go
In Regent's Park, three weeks ago,
And came all Cantona with me
As I was stopping for a pee,
And murmured silently (as we dogs do),
'Ooh, 'allo ducky. Look at you!'

I thought, 'Now this is ultra brash:
If I can't have a quiet slash
Without some poncey, foreign prat
Delivering insulting chat,
(Forgive me if I play the ham)
I'm not the dog I think I am.
I'd give that twerpish mummy's pet
A lesson he would not forget . . .'

I didn't bite his ear, as such;
In fact, I didn't even touch
A single, pouffed-up, well-groomed hair.
But this was neither here nor there,
For all his saddo owner cared.
She swore that all my teeth were bared
And buried in her darling's flesh,
Like scorpions in Marrakech.

She swore like a Kilkenny cat,
And promised this and threatened that,
And, blow me down, went on to hector
A Royal Parks police inspector,
Who said, 'This conduct will not do.
What is the dog world coming to
When pets like little chummy here
Must live their life in hate and fear?'

So now I'm always on the lead
Because some twerpish foreign breed

Of thicko, supercilious mutt
Can't keep its stupid cake-hole shut.

I do not like you, small Maltese,
You canine Mephistopheles.

Back Seat Diver

Ulysses, soaked and muddy,
Stood panting by the car,
And Dickie, his best buddy,
Was smoking a cigar.
He reached into his pocket,
And, fumbling for the key,
Stepped forward to unlock it.
The ancient Ford Capri
Was not in good condition,
It had been in many wars,
Cursed with a bum ignition
And stained by filthy paws.
The locks were very sticky;
They'd baffle any thief.
They always baffled Dickie;
It beggared all belief.

The Merc behind could not have been
More pristine if it tried;
Such automotive pedigree
Is very hard to hide.
A trophy wife in fur and jeans
Climbed out, went round the back;
She didn't give a row of beans
For Dickie in his mac.

She opened up the nearside door
To let her Yorkie out.
She yelled, she shrieked, she screamed, she swore –
'Get out! Get out! Get out!'

The terrier was still inside,
And screaming even louder;
And next to him sat Ulysses –
No dog could have looked prouder.

Odds and Sods

I'm not a well-bred animal;
I'm made of bits and bobs.
My pedigree is minimal;
I'm not one of the nobs.

My dad's a small Chihuahua;
My mother is a Beagle –
Embarrassing for poor Mama
Who's really rather regal.

They sold me as a Cheagle,
The people in North Wales.
To do so's not illegal:
They've no need to tell tales.

They breed all kinds of mongrels
(Or hybrids, I should say),
And no one ever grumbles,
Or brings them back next day.

They give them funny, made-up names
To make them seem more real.
Like silly words in Scrabble games,
Some sound all too surreal.

My neighbours have a Cockerpoo –
Half poodle and half spaniel.
They found him somewhere north of Crewe
And christened him Nathaniel.

One can feel quite a fool, it's true,
And anyone can knock.
But better far a Cockerpoo
Than be called Poodlecock.

An Easter Tale

While walking out one April day,
I met a dog along the way –
Light brown and black, both ears well pricked,
And long pink tongue that licked and licked.

The sea below was flecked with white;
A soft wind blew; the sky was bright.
In all, a day to make one smile
At Easter on a small Greek isle.

We sat and talked, the dog and I;
He showed no fear; he wasn't shy.
So loving did he seem to be,
I felt as if he'd chosen me.

Though why, I'd not the faintest clue;
He'd come, it seemed, from out the blue –
A mutt that showed no want or need,
Whose eyes did not demand or plead.
Quite self-contained, no pampered pet,
A stray, like countless thousands, yet . . .

As if dark clouds had crossed the sun,
The day began to seem less fun.
Stray pets abroad can be sheer hell –
Like matey guests in one's hotel,
Who somehow fail to get it right
And know what time to say goodnight.

I sat; he sat; I tried to pray
In hope that he'd just go away.
Fat chance: I strode a good mile on,
But still the damned fool hadn't gone.

No collar, not a soul in view;
No place that I could take him to;
No local vet where he could stay;
No Greek-style RSPCA . . .

And then a miracle occurred,
When somewhere way below I heard
Faint sounds of laughter; high-pitched shrieks –
The sort that's often made by Greeks.

And suddenly there hove in sight
Beneath a cliff just to my right,
A little village with a square.
I walked him down and left him there.

He looked away to check a smell;
I turned and, like a young gazelle,
Up through the sun-baked street I ran,
A cowardly and haunted man.

Safe on the cliff, I stood, and there,
Alone in the deserted square,
He wandered round from side to side,
Then lifted up his head and cried.

No child lost on a shopping spree
Could howl as half as loud as he.
I came at last. 'I'm here,' I said.
He stopped and gently turned his head.

I smacked my thighs and waved an arm;
He seemed unreasonably calm.
'It's me,' I said. 'Come on! Let's go!'
Stretched out a hand and crouched down low.

His eyes were cold; his ears drooped;
His back, once straight, seemed sadly stooped.
'You had your chance,' he seemed to say,
And turned and slowly walked away.

Waste Not, Want Not

Most dogs are quite carnivorous;
They like a meaty tin.
My Wheaten is omnivorous –
He'll shovel most things in.
An ordinary Dublin street
Is food and drink to him:
Whatever lies beneath his feet,
However grey and grim –
Discarded bits of pizza crust,
Old fag ends, scraps of paper –
For Corky every walk is just
A non-stop gourmet caper.

It seemed that nothing made him ill –
A well-filled baby's nappy
Was caviar to him, until
The time he felt so crappy
He didn't want to walk, or play,
And seemed distinctly *piano* –
As dopey as he did the day
He drank a large Cinzano.

At half past six he coughed and choked,
And swallowed like a porpoise.
I really thought he might have croaked –
A most un-Roman *corpus*.
He's going to be sick, I thought,
And looked round for a bucket.
But no, too late! 'Twas all for naught.
I thought, well, frankly, Bother.
Then up it came and out it spewed –
A shapeless lump of horror,
Quite undigested and unchewed,
Dark brown with slime. Begorrah!
It couldn't be! It was! Good grief!
From some deep, dark recess –
My favourite Swiss lace handkerchief!
A miracle, no less!

A careless man who casts aside
A pearl of wondrous price,
And sees it vanish on the tide
Would dare not risk it twice.
I took the stinking fabric and
I washed it through and through,
And ironed it with a loving hand.
It looked as good as new.

That evening when I took it out –
As white as driven snow,
And frothy as a water spout
On Lake Ontario –
A waggish woman in a hat
Said, 'That looks nice and clean!'
I thought, 'You wouldn't say that
If you knew where it had been!'

Dachshund, Dachshund
Über Alles

When they sank the *Lusitania*
A year into the War,
It launched a worldwide mania
For giving Fritz what for.

They ditched the German Shepherd,
And called it an Alsatian –
Though, rather like the leopard,
It maintained its pigmentation.

But, being less exotic,
With their funny outsize feet,
It was thought quite patriotic
To kick Dachshunds in the street.

Forget the fearsome Pit Bull
And other breeds that fight;
The sausage dog is fitful
And much likelier to bite.

Well, is it any wonder?
We're really all to blame.
It only takes one blunder
To ruin a dog's name.

Dog Beneath the Skin

It isn't my fault I'm a Mastiff,
And I'm called the Incredible Hulk.
I may look like a bundle of mischief –
Not surprisingly, given my bulk.

Kev my owner's a serious hard man:
Six foot six and a football pitch wide.
You need to be tough as a yard man,
And you need a tough dog at your side.

This is where I must make a confession
That I'm not quite the chap for the job.
I'm relying on you for discretion
When I say that I feel a right knob.

Every thunderstorm turns me to jelly,
And when I hear the smallest dog bark,
I look sad and lie flat on my belly –
I'm the weediest hound in the park.

Like the Cowardly Lion in the movie
Of *The Wizard of Oz*, I pretend
To be fearless and gung-ho and groovy,
Yet at heart I'm just Dorothy's friend.

I've made chums with a neighbourhood poodle,
Who, like me, has no great urge to hack it,
And talk big and indulge in flapdoodle.
(And I don't half begrudge his pink jacket.)

As things stand, Kev has no cause to doubt me;
I'll continue to look the real thing.
Just as long as some bitch doesn't out me,
I'm as tough as a rare piece of Ming.

Up Wind

I'm not what you might call a flatulent type,
Though boiled cabbage can get me going;
And I have to admit that occasionally tripe
Will produce wind without my knowing.

But, more often than not – do you know what?
When one's owners complain of a pong,
It isn't their dogs that have put up a blot;
They're the ones who are most in the wrong.

Telly Pug

Hieronymus, a perky Pug,
Was something of a telly bug.
A thoroughly devoted pet,
His true love was the TV set.
The moment that the screen turned bright,
He'd think, 'Aha. Well, that's all right,'
And hop up on a little stool,
And sit there motionless, and drool.

He didn't care for *Downton Abbey*,
Which left him curiously crabby;
And bored with yet another bake-off,
He'd give a glance and quickly take off.
He never fancied Simon Cowell –
That voice alone would make him howl;
And frankly he would rather die
Than waste one minute on *QI*.

Most documentaries were a drag,
But nature programmes *were* his bag.
When lions leapt and zebras quailed,
His concentration never failed.

His joy was *One Man and His Dog* –
No viewer could be more agog.
Kate Humble was his heroine –
A lovely girl, a lovely grin.
On tiptoe, nose against the screen,
He'd goggle at the rural scene
With beady eyes and heavy breath,
Like Banquo's Ghost at poor Macbeth.

His great ambition was to drive
A bunch of sheep, say four or five,
No more, across a hillside, then
Enclose them in a makeshift pen.

The day they took the programme off
He fell into a deep, dark trough.
Most dogs would be content to sleep,
But not a pug whose joy was sheep.
So now the show was on the shelf,
He planned to have a go himself,
And re-live the bucolic thrills
Of dogs at work on sunlit hills.

The minds of mutts we cannot plumb;
Their urges are extremely rum;
So there should be no real surprise
At what may suddenly arise
When instinct more than common sense
Can seize a dog and cause offence,
As happened in the park one day,
Where nursery school kids come to play,
And throw soft balls and run about,
And let off steam and scream and shout,
And fall face down in nasty thistles,
While teachers wave and blow loud whistles.

A game of tag was in full flow
When, like an arrow from a bow,
A small black shape comes tearing up,
No larger than a spaniel pup,
And suddenly, with puffs and grunts
And lots of snuffling, confronts
The children and, with furious haste,

Has all of them securely placed
Within a sort of fairy ring,
Ruled by a would-be sheepdog king,
Masquerading as a Pug,
Eyes goggling, and rather smug.

A passer-by said, 'I'm a fan
Of country sports with dog and man;
But, frankly, after watching that,
I'd really rather use a cat.'

The Dog and Duck

You don't have to be Konrad Lorenz
To know some dogs have no common sense.
Our spaniel called Matty
Could turn really batty,
And sometimes cause massive expense.

When she felt she'd been treated too hard,
She would pick up this duck in the yard
(The duck would play dead –
It was frightfully well bred)
And present it with faint disregard.

A Springer we once had called Willow,
As if caught in a mild peccadillo,
Would take one of her litter
And carefully fit her
Most lovingly under my pillow.

A Collie we knew called Charlene
Did the weirdest thing we've ever seen:
At the first hint of thunder
She'd stagger and blunder
Straight inside the washing machine.

We had a Saluki called Jane,
Who would sing like Madonna in pain.
There wasn't much tune
To whatever she'd croon,
Though it could have been 'Lili Marlene'.

Last Post

Not a sound was heard, not a word was said,
As old Jim to the vet was transported;
From the moment they carried him out on his bed,
He was pretty damned sure he had bought it.

He hadn't been feeling too good for some while,
Or in much of a mood for long walkies.
They'd tell friends he was looking quite well, and they'd
    smile,
But he knew they were telling them porkies.

He had had a good innings with Julian and Fee
In a Kensington flat and in Norfolk,
In a smart barn conversion near Wells-next-the-Sea;
He thanked heaven they hadn't been poor folk.

He was not a great gun dog, he had to confess,
And the booms and the bangs made him quiver;
He felt far more at home and quite free of all stress
On the banks of a gentle trout river.

He had never done anything worthy of fame,
Such as rescuing swimmers and stuff,
But no one could say that old Jim wasn't brave,
Least of all when the going got tough.

And it didn't get tougher than facing one's end,
With one's owners tight-lipped in the front.
This was no way to treat a lifelong friend,
And he felt quite put out, to be blunt.

As they pulled up outside the vet's handsome front
    door,
He felt sure he detected a sniffle,
And he thought, 'As behaviour goes, this is quite poor.
Let's get on. I am tired of this piffle.'

He lay still and soft-eyed as the needle went in,
And the moment they'd dreaded soon passed.
Jim had died as he lived, a great dog without sin,
Uncomplaining and loyal to the last.

Horse and Hound

When Susie moved to Gloucestershire,
It was no serious loss to her.
Three decades' worth of city grime
Had made her realise it was time
To seek new pastures, breathe fresh air –
It really didn't matter where,
As long as there were trees and grass,
Like-minded neighbours (middle class),
Who understood the simple life,
Light years away from stress and strife.

For divorcées of twenty years,
Arcadian England holds no fears.
A handsome house, a 4 x 4,
A Scottie dog, a Labrador,
Surrounding fields, two walks a day:
Her life was one long month of May.

I say two walks, though not for Suze;
The very thought gave her the blues.
She'd never been mad keen on sport:
Why walk when you can drive? she thought.

For her there is no nicer treat
Than sitting in the driving seat,
And moving at a stately pace
Behind an energetic brace
Of healthy, happy carefree chaps
Who never show signs of collapse,
While madam sits there on the phone,
Like Cleopatra on her throne.
And, as the dogs cavort, she natters
About this, that, and other matters,
And pauses for a sip of beer
While drifting off to Borsetshire.

Now Jock, the bustling, bright-eyed Scottie,
Was well behaved and never grotty,
Except when faced with serious threats
To life and limb from other pets.
It wasn't for himself he cared
So much as for such fools as dared
To put his owner in harm's way,
And treat her to a bad-hair day –
As happened when the local hunt
Foregathered once outside the front
Of Susie's house for stirrup cups
And chaff, and chat, and 'giddy-ups';
And Susie, who was in the know,
Guessed just which way the hunt would go,
And took her dogs elsewhere, quite sure
That hounds would never find their spoor.

So you can picture her surprise
When, busy making up her eyes,
She was confronted by the sight
Of hounds and horses in full flight,
Breasting the stubbled field ahead.
What should she do? Sit still? Reverse?
She swallowed, she began to curse;
The dogs were nowhere to be seen –
Her brain had turned to plasticine.
She didn't often lose the plot,
But now she felt a real clot.

A small shape darted from the right,
Compact and low and black as night.
It rocketed towards the hunt,
Prepared, like David, to confront
Goliath and the charging horde,
And put his army to the sword.

'My God, it's Jock!' squeaked Suze at last;
She couldn't move, she stared aghast
As he tore on, his tail held high
Into the jaws of death. Goodbye?

But no. He stopped. He stood. He glowered,
Like some Leviathan empowered.
He didn't budge; he didn't flinch;
He dared them to go one more inch ...

The horses jam their hooves right in;
They're all in a most frightful spin;
The huntsmen are in disarray;
The hounds begin to whine and bay.
The hunt comes to a grinding halt;
It isn't anybody's fault –
Except that one small dog called Jock,
Had caused this most almighty shock,
For no good reason other than
The duty of a dog to man.

A Bus Pass Named Desire: Romances for the Young at Heart

Introduction

One of the great stage successes of the 1950s in London and New York was *The Boy Friend* by Sandy Wilson. A comic pastiche of musical shows of the 1920s, it is set on the French Riviera and concerns the romantic shenanigans of the girls at Madame Dubonnet's School for Young Ladies.

I won't even begin to describe the labyrinthine plot, except to say that in Act 3 a silly old fool called Lord Brockhurst sings 'It's Never Too Late to Fall in Love' with a particularly flirty young lady named Dulcie.

'It's never too late to have a fling,' he warbles. 'For autumn is just as nice as spring. And it's never too late to fall in love.' To which she responds with the immortal line 'Boop-a-Doop, Boop-a-Doop, Boop-a-Doop' before going on to agree that 'One never drinks the wine that's new. The old wine tastes much nicer.'

Time was when a man of advancing years or more could fall for a gel young enough to be his daughter and be considered as little more than an amusing cove and something of a goer. As for the Dulcies of the day, well ... there have always been young women who go for the older man.

In these sterner times, any man over the age of fifty expressing romantic sentiments to a young lady – however frivolously – runs a serious risk of being asked to resign from his club, if not worse.

On that occasion, the noble troubadour – caught in mid-warble by his wife – got off with a sharp wigging. Fair enough. Silly old fool. He should have been keeping *cave*.

But who is to say that after a certain age men should no longer be allowed to admire youth and beauty? And not only to admire them, but to express their sentiments in no uncertain terms? An older woman can be as flirtatious with a younger man as she wants, and no one thinks the worse of her.

Love can strike anyone at any time, regardless of age or sexual inclination. Falling in love is not a prerogative of the young. There are any number of members of both sexes at different moments in their lives who find love for the first time, or the second, or even the third, following a death or a divorce – sometimes with a younger partner, sometimes with someone of their own age, occasionally with someone he or she has known in an earlier life.

Love that flowers late in life is often the strongest and most enduring, and it is in celebration of such love that these poems have been written.

There is a school of thought that would have one believe that the older one is when one falls in love, the greater the chance of making a pig's ear of things – in the early stages, anyway – partly because even if one manages to pluck one's youthful chat-up lines from the sludge of memory, the chances are one will have forgotten what to do next.

On the whole, though, most discover that by the time they reach middle age and beyond, they are more than capable of taking awkward moments in their stride and rising above them.

At all events, this book should help to reassure its silver-haired readers that not only do more and more people find love in later life, but that – often against all the odds – most of them manage to sustain it. Which is why the short stories in this collection (for that is what these poems are, in disguise) are as much about keeping marriages going as they are about heading for it.

As the years go by, contentment becomes more and more a condition to be cherished, and couples find it in many different forms: in shared pleasures at the bridge table, on the tennis court, in the herbaceous border, on a bicycle made for two, or simply in warm companionship.

Mind you, few manage to keep their marriages going without driving each other potty from time to time. The grit in the oyster is usually some trivial and inexplicable quirk of behaviour, such as disappearing upstairs just as lunch is on the table, or repeating long-winded anecdotes, or insisting on wearing clothes that should long since have found their proper home in the local household waste recycling centre.

But what ensures that a marriage remains on an even keel more effectively than the odd spot of brisk bickering?

Those who have happy memories of musical comedies such as *The Boy Friend* (i.e. the generation for whom this book is mainly intended) will not need reminding that what made these shows such hits in the gloomy, black-and-white days of the 1950s was the lightness of touch of the plots, the music, and, above all, the high-spirited lyrics.

This collection is not without its occasional moments of sadness, of disappointment and of regret; but a light touch has prevailed which, like Sandy Wilson's, might help to raise a few spirits – and a few smiles – on St Valentine's Day and beyond.

All the Wrong Moves

When an older man starts courting after too long on
     the shelf,
He often finds he's lost the art of being just himself.
He bumbles and he fumbles like a teenage debutant
Who is trying to act like Brosnan in a fancy
     restaurant.
He's forgotten all his chat-up lines, yet still cannot stop
     talking,
And telling awful jokes, not knowing he's a dead man
     walking.
All too often, basic hygiene has a tendency to suffer;
BO and halitosis are sure signs of an old buffer.
And unattractive habits can abruptly raise their head
When an oldie has his mind on rather better things –
     like bed.

When Dave Trout took a fancy to the widow from
     next door,
He asked her round for dinner – and perchance a little
     more.
The table glowed with candlelight, the champagne was
     on ice;
She looked around and ate a crisp and said, 'Well, this
     is nice.'

The prawn cocktail was a triumph and the steak just
    hit the spot;
The Merlot slipped down easily, they both drank quite
    a lot.
The atmosphere was warming up, the time was almost
    right
For Dave to make his move like any parfait, gentle
    knight.
With coffee and an After Eight he felt he couldn't miss.
As he placed them on the table, he leaned forward for
    a kiss,
And tripped and spilt the coffee and got into such
    a flap,
She ended with a coffee-flavoured toupee in her lap.

306

Anyone for Tennis?

John Betjeman was not a man to pussyfoot around;
His penchant for athletic girls is generally
    renowned.
His singles with Miss Hunter Dunn held keen
    young players breathless;
Their late-night car park tryst was told in verse one
    might call deathless.
That great big mountainous sports girl, Pam, was
    passionately adored;
The tall Olympic girl had young John well and truly
    floored.
But callow love will have its day and beauty fades
    too soon;
The days grow cold, and hair turns grey, and
    autumn's far from June.
Late-flowering lust is all that men can hope for in
    old age;
The rapture that they felt in youth is oft replaced
    by rage.
To fall in love when young was just like falling off
    a log,
And no amount of skill can teach new tricks to an
    old dog.

A moment of flirtation that might launch a
  thousand ships
Has now become the subject of embarrassment and
  quips.
The girls one played long rallies with were sweet,
  but could be tough,
And secretly we knew that we were not quite up to
  snuff.
It mattered less who won or lost than who could
  catch the girl;
With luck the score became love-all, and life one
  glorious whirl.
But now that we are old and fat and liable to sweat,
There's little chance that we'll once more find love
  across the net.
We will not know that thrill again; we'll never feel
  the same;
But those girls are our partners now and we have
  won the game!

The Perils and Pleasures of Marrying a Much Younger Woman

You make me feel so old.
You make me feel like blue cheese mould.
And every time you call my name,
I'm just another old retainer type.

The moment that you sigh,
I want to fly to Paraguay.
I want to buy a big straw hat
And vanish under that.

You make me
Feel just like a silly old crock,
Toddling round the garden,
Looking like a washed-out, well-darned sock.

You make me feel so whacked.
You make me feel like a child that's been smacked,
A star who's been hacked,
Ancient Rome on the day it was sacked.

But though you're only thirty-two,
I feel so lucky that I'm hitched to you,
'Cos your love for me's pure gold.

My Love is Like a Red, Red Nose

Now Bob is not a soppy date,
Like some blokes are at fifty-eight,
Who kiss and cuddle, bill and coo,
And send their loved ones billets-doux,
And goggle at them day and night,
Like lovebirds on a wedding night,
And call them silly, baby names,
And make up silly, baby games.

Yet he is a romantic soul,
Who strikes the right notes on the whole
When anniversaries and such
Demand the right, romantic touch.
Then Interflora get the nod –
He needs no hint; he needs no prod.
His feelings are beyond reproach.
(He once bought Phyl a diamond brooch.)

Time was, when he was courting her,
The least excuse would be a spur
To yet more touching little signs
Of love – and one was Valentine's.

A card was sent, unsigned of course,
Adorned with hearts to reinforce
His ardour and undying passion
In what was then a sure-fire fashion.
Old Errol Flynn in all his glory
Could not have pitched a better story.
But that was then, and well past fifty,
Bob's amorous skills are far less nifty.
No married man of middle age
Should need to rattle Cupid's cage.
And yet he dared not disappoint
By putting Phyl's nose out of joint.
A simple gesture, nothing grand:
The lightest hint – she'd understand
That Bob would love her, come what may,
Though flesh might sag and hair turn grey.

If men Bob's age can't be Byronic,
The next best bet is be ironic.
And so he turned, as many do,
In search of a romantic coup
In gift departments, catalogues –
The natural home for underdogs
Not blessed with much poetic thought.

He very, very nearly bought
A rather pretty, heart-shaped mug
That doubled as a coffee jug,
But lost his head, one has to say,

And plumped for Anti-Nagging Spray –
Quite witty and a bit of fun,
That couldn't offend anyone . . .

Phyl simply never got the joke.
The memory still makes him choke.
He doesn't see her much now she
Has moved to sunny Brightlingsea.
Her card stands open by his bed:
A single heart in vivid red.
A little faded, dog-eared too,
Signed 'All my love, from You-Know-Who'.

One-Minute Stand

When Sam put his profile on Tinder,
He felt sure he'd find true love with Linda.
She looked just like his ex,
But she wanted odd sex.
'Not at my age,' said Sam, and he binned her.

Nanny

I fell in love with Nanny Bree
When I was seventeen,
And she was two years more than me.
My goodness, was I keen!

She came to work one summer's day
For John and Barbara Foad,
Who owned a house called Tannoch Brae,
The biggest in our road.
Their son was my best friend at school;
His Christian name was Sunny –
The pure embodiment of cool,
And very, very funny.

He had this little sister, Prue –
An after-thought, he said:
A boring little blister who
Would never go to bed.
And so they hired Nanny Bree,
Fair-haired and born in Fowey;
She changed their lives dramatically,
And filled the house with joy.

One hot day by the swimming pool
I found her in the nude.
I went bright red, I felt a fool.
'I hope you're not a prude,'
She said. 'I'm not the girl I seem –
Some nymphomaniac.
You see that tube of suntan cream?
Please rub it on my back.'

I've never tried to put on airs,
Or blow my you-know-what.
I closed my eyes and said my prayers,
Then slightly lost the plot.
I also lost my khaki shorts,
And rather more than that.
I had no time for modest thoughts;
I fell, and that was that.

We loved and laughed all summer long,
And no one ever knew –
Though how can anything be wrong
When hearts are young and true?
We'd make love and we'd dance a lot
And meet in secret places.
Like Guinevere and Lancelot,
We knew full well what grace is.

But all too soon the school gates closed;
I wished that I could die.
She loved me still, as I supposed.
I wrote, but no reply.
My agony grew more intense
As day dragged after day.
Without her, life made no more sense;
I thought of turning gay.

School broke up just before I did.
I called; she wasn't there.
I went round in one final bid,
To find she didn't care.
As autumn winds cool summer's heat
And green leaves turn to gold,
So even smiles can seem less sweet
And kisses pale and cold.

I never knew, she never said
That love can be so cruel.
My life moved on, all hope had fled –
No thoughts of a renewal.

She nannied on for many years –
Another generation
Of little beasts and little dears
For her consideration.

At thirty-two I married Nell;
Three children came, and then,
Blow me, while playing bridge, she fell
For some rich twerp called Ben.

While playing golf one January,
I heard the Foads were dead.
A service in their memory
Was held in Maidenhead.

I didn't recognise one face;
I thought, 'This is uncanny.'
I kept my cool and found a place
Beside somebody's granny.
'I'm sorry, I am rather late ...'
We smiled at one another.
I tried my best to concentrate.
She looked quite like my mother.

I looked around the jam-packed church;
Had I got the right day?
And then my stomach gave a lurch,
For there, not far away,
Sat Bree, her hair just touched with grey,
Her face a little fatter.

The years quite simply slipped away.
What does a grey hair matter?

Was she the reason I had come?
(The mighty organ thundered.)
To salvage just the tiniest crumb,
Of self-respect? I wondered.

The drinks were in the pub next door.
I hugged my friend; he wept.
'As pals go, I've been pretty poor –
Uncaring and inept.'

We talked a while of this and that,
Remembering our lost youth:
The day we tried to sell the cat,
And found a mammoth's tooth.
I told him I had spotted Bree;
She'd hardly changed at all –
At least as far as I could see,
And I was still in thrall.

'I don't know what you're telling me;
I haven't got a clue.
It wasn't Bree,' he said, 'as she
Was sitting next to you.'

My mouth was dry, my face was hot,
My mind was truly boggled.
I stood there like the wife of Lot,
Immobilised, and goggled.
'But she was ... That was never Bree ...
She never gave a hint ...
The only thing she offered me
Was one small Trebor mint.'

'She couldn't stay,' he said. 'She went,
But asked to be remembered.'
I stood there like a non-event –
A tree that's been dismembered.

'She recognised you straight away.
She thought you looked depressed.
The only thing that she would say
Was "Nanny does know best."'

Newly Weds

St Valentine's the day for chaps to get down on one
      knee,
And put their hands upon their hearts and say,
      'Please marry me.'
To modern tastes such ancient rites may verge on
      the pedantic,
But gesture-wise, it's hard to think of any more
      romantic.

So when Jack popped the question to his childhood
      sweetheart, Pat,
She said, 'I don't believe it, love. You could have
      knocked me flat.
To think we've been together now for nearly half
      our lives.
That's more than you can say for many husbands,
      and their wives.'

'We could have carried on,' he said, 'as pals, the way
      we were.
It isn't right to live in sin, but humans often err.
Yet now I feel the time has come to do the proper
      thing,
And make it all official-like, with champagne and
      a ring.'

'I'd like to marry you,' she said. 'I'd like to be your
      wife,
And share what I am sure will be a long and happy
      life.
Let's celebrate – I tell you what, I'll go and make
      some tea.
Here, help me up and then I'll try and lift you off
      your knee.'

They married in the local church, then partied on
      till one;
They drank champagne and danced, and said
      they'd never had such fun.
They left aboard a vintage Rolls. 'I won't
      exaggerate,'
Said Pat. 'You don't look much like Wills, but I feel
      just like Kate!'

On honeymoon in Seaview House near Eastbourne
      in the wet,
Jack said, 'I'm not a gambling man, but I'm
      prepared to bet
That we're the only couple here who've been
      prepared to wait
And marry when one's ninety-six, and the other's
      ninety-eight.'

Star Quality

A big surprise for Jenny Parr
Was realising she was a star.
It's not the sort of thing you do
When you're a gran of eighty-two,
And live a life of widowed bliss
In Norfolk, five miles north of Diss.

But Jenny was no aged slouch,
Stretched out upon a comfy couch –
A wrinkled Venus of Urbino,
Immobilised by food and vino.

One minute she was Mrs Parr,
As far removed from brouhaha
As Trappist nuns in olden days

Who'd sit alone in cells and gaze
With holy thoughts and silent prayer
At empty brick walls rude and bare.

Next thing she knew, she got a call
From someone who said, 'My name's Paul.
I'm ringing from the BBC.
I see that back in '93
You gave a talk on *Woman's Hour*
About the strength of housewife power.
It seems that you caused quite a stir,
And we in Arts and Ent concur
That you would be the perfect choice
(And, dare I say, the perfect voice)
As Household Goddess *de nos jours* –
A force to reckon with, we're sure.'

Her daughter said, 'Go for it, Mum!
You'll only sit there on your bum.
God knows, you've got star quality,
And common sense and jollity.
We need a new face on our screens
As charismatic as the Queen's.'

She did the pilot, got the gig.
In truth she thought it infra dig,
But played the game and took the dosh
For being, frankly, nice and posh,
As Jennifer, the female judge

On TV's latest hit, *The Drudge* –
A contest between would-be chars
Who work in houses, flats and bars,
And hope to prove their household skills
On kitchen floors and window sills,
And daunting piles of washing-up,
To win the much prized Daily Cup,
And punch the air while millions cheer
The newly crowned Char of the Year.

Her co-judge was a bloke called Ed,
Who she felt wasn't too well bred,
But had an oddly peasant charm –
The sort you might find on a farm:
A Mellors type (plus aftershave)
Who makes old ladies misbehave.

The erstwhile host of *Who Wants Fame?*
(A sort of talent-show-cum-game),
He'd got the looks; she'd got the class.
His vowels were hairy; hers cut glass.
They made the ideal TV pair
(With curiously contrasting hair),
Who made the viewing figures sing
While tills in hardware stores went 'Ting!'
And Jenny's heart did much the same:
A bonus for a doughty dame.

Now Jenny is a superstar:
She's been on *Who Do You Think You Are?*
Her bank account is into millions;
Her Twitter feed is read by zillions.
For services to charity,
The Queen gave her the OBE.
In public she's pursued by hordes;
She'll soon be in the House of Lords.
From Torquay to the Isle of Skye,
She's better known than Stephen Fry.

To top it all, at eighty-two,
She's found true love with someone who,
(Despite a yawning gap in age
The size of the Palladium stage)
Has given her a real buzz.

'Well, handsome is as handsome does,'
She told a writer from the *Mail*.
'Do I look doddery and frail?
I'm no spring chicken, I'll admit,
And some may think that I'm a twit.
But life is short, and can be merry;
Just look at my friend Mary Berry.
I may be old, but far from dead.
You don't believe me? Just ask Ed!'

Crossroads

'Do you want to come up for a nightcap?'
She said with a knowing look.
I was tired and fancied a light nap,
With a nice cup of tea and a book.

As I ruminate on the hereafter,
I remember that moment with Beth.
Did I turn down a lifetime of laughter
And love? Or a fate worse than death?

I Say Potato and You Say Potato

For lovers strolling in the park
A little sport can be a lark.
But Fred was taking quite a chance
By asking Ginger, 'Shall we dance?'
For all too soon it dawned on Fred
That their new love might soon be dead,
Since neither of them could agree
(At least as far as they could see)

On how to utter every word
The way that he or she preferred.
And rather than compare and scoff,
They almost called the whole thing off.

Disputes on good pronunciation
Can lead to fierce denunciation.
And silly things that drive wives potty
Can make their husbands think they're dotty.
'She has this most annoying giggle.'
'He has a tendency to niggle.'
'She never hears a word I say.'
'I think he think he's Ai Weiwei . . .'
There's talk of twits and hypocrites,
And even splits and lawyers' writs.

Some battles lovers never win;
They take reproval on the chin.
And friends are brought in on the joke
As couples dig and prod and poke,
And bore them with the latest quirk,
And how their other half's a berk.

But lovers love to fight and bicker.
Like thieves, a good row makes them thicker.
There's nothing wrong with getting cross
So long as no one gives a toss.

The Longings of Youth

At public school in '53
Tom played against the MCC,
And caught the eye of one small boy
Who soon became his light and joy.
He never spoke his love, just looked,
Though he was well and truly hooked.
When girls were not there for a fling,
A crush must be the next best thing.

Not even girls at teenage dances,
And sweaty palms and meaning glances,
And kisses with a blonde called Dinah
Could melt his love for Simpkins Minor.

A year off with the VSO
In Java and then Borneo
Gave little time for love, or games:
All Cupid's darts had lost their aims.
And friendship with a Dayak cook
Was warm enough, but never took.

A don at Cambridge held his hand,
And murmured softly, 'I have planned
A walking tour in Italy.
You'd be most welcome, if you're free.
The trip's on me. To tell the truth,
Age always travels best with youth.
The older man is wise and knowing;
The younger one can keep him going.'

Tom thought about it hard and long,
And gravely weighed up right and wrong.
Was this a chance he shouldn't miss?
An undiscovered life of bliss?

But then he met a girl called Becks
And learnt the meaning of great sex.

Though love played very little part,
She made him laugh and touched his heart;
And any thoughts of donnish travel
Were bound to tarnish and unravel.

In '69 Tom married Jane
And never once looked back again.
Retired now, they live in Kent –
A white-haired pair who represent
The very best of English life:
An upright husband, faithful wife,
In love, whatever 'in love' means;
In no doubt which way each one leans.

These days men hug and often kiss.
Does Tom, one wonders, ever miss
Those wild romantic schoolboy crushes,
Or should one save the poor chap's blushes?

The Food of Love

Shall I compare thee to my chicken pie?
Thou art as tender and as succulent.
Love, like beauty, is in the beholder's eye –
Or was it my spiced slow roast duck you meant?

Love in an Old Climate

The naughtiest girl in Heygate House
Was Arabella Vogelzand.
Appearance-wise a timid mouse,
She played a very cunning hand.

Retirement homes were not her bag.
Confined there under strict duress,
She thought the whole thing was a drag –
Except when planning to transgress.

Well-meaning men would patronise
And treat her like a backward child,
And all too soon, to their surprise,
Discover someone slightly wild.

The vicar visited one day –
A nice young chap, all smiles and teeth.
She said, 'You look as if you're gay.
Or are you all man underneath?'

She organised some kitchen bridge
And ballroom dancing in the hall.
For most it was a privilege,
But Bella had a real ball.

One inmate nearly had a stroke
When Bella grinned and rubbed his knees
And said, 'I'd really love a poke.
Could you perhaps oblige me, please?'

She fell one day and gave her hip
A really rather nasty bash.
The doctor came. 'I'd better strip,'
She said, and did so in a flash.

One day the janitor, called Reed,
Said, 'Anything you need, sweetheart?'
She winked. 'There's just one thing I need,
And you'd do nicely for a start.'

Her daughter came, so did her son.
'There've been a few complaints,' they said.
'What's wrong with just a little fun?'
She asked. 'I'll very soon be dead.'

It seemed that not one carer knew
That old men long to have a fling.
Not even Matron had a clue
That care home inmates sometimes swing.

So when she heard a man called Ray
Had spent the night in Bella's bed,
And planned to stay there for the day,
Her heart was filled with fearful dread.

She found them locked there in mid-kiss,
Till Bella flashed a wicked grin.
'This isn't what you think it is.
I'm giving Ray an aspirin.'

The Real Thing?

Young Tim, rehearsing Hamlet, was a dedicated
     pro;
He knew as much about the part as anyone could
     know.
One thing, however, puzzled him about the gloomy
     Dane:
Does Hamlet love Ophelia, like Tarzan loved young
     Jane?
Is she a friend, no more, no less? A mere platonic
     chum?
Or is there more between them? Do they ever once
     succumb?
He buttonholed Polonius, who was very much old
     school.
'I need your input, Johnny; I don't want to look a
     fool.
Ophelia and Hamlet – are they having an affair?'
He said, 'They were when I played him in
     Weston-super-Mare.'

Secret Love

The greatest joy of George's life
(Apart, of course, from his dear wife)
Was his young grandson, Valentine,
A lively little chap of nine.

Now Val was not like other boys;
He had no interest in toys,
Or playing football in the wet,
Or socialising on the net.

While science held no mystery
His passion was for history –
Specifically for World War Two,
Of which George knew a thing or two.
A London baby in the Blitz,
He kept young Valentine in fits
Of laughter, mixed with solemn awe,
With tales of schoolboy derring-do
And slightly unhinged masters who,
When somewhat overcome by booze,
Would vent their wrath on cheeky youths.

Hour after hour they'd sit and talk,
And often do so on a walk.
'The attic!' then would come the cry,
And, like two schoolboys on the sly,
They'd slip upstairs and there they'd spend
What seemed to Val like hours on end,
Exploring Grandpa's secret hoard
Of childhood treasures he had stored
In nooks and crannies out of sight
From Granny's fierce, relentless fight
To chuck out what she saw as junk
From every chest and drawer and trunk –
Frayed shirts and ties and golf-club socks
And ski gloves squirrelled in a box,
And pullovers with friendly holes,
And slippers looking like dead moles.

But thus far she had not discovered,
Concealed inside a dusty cupboard,
His stash of childhood souvenirs –
The erstwhile envy of his peers:
A prep school cap with faded stripes,
His father's rack of favourite pipes,
Lead soldiery of every rank,
A model of a Churchill tank,
A single strand of Nelson's hair,
A letter signed by Rupert Bear,
And cigarette cards by the score
Of modern naval craft, and more –
Old film stars with forgotten names,
And cricketers from pre-war games,
Sea fishes, dogs and railway trains,
And limousines and weather vanes.
They'd sit there in the musty gloom
Like students in a reading room,
Discussing every card in turn
With almost scholarly concern,
With Grandpa crouching on his knees,
Dispensing dubious expertise.

The only headache in this lark
Was keeping Granny in the dark,
For fear she'd think dear George a chump
And take the whole lot to the dump.
So when they found the cupboard door
Wide open, and the next thing saw

That everything had disappeared,
They thought it was just as they'd feared:
The game was up, their race was run;
From then on life would be less fun.
They'd have to find new things to do,
Like going to the London Zoo.

They felt their spirit levels fall
As they descended to the hall,
Preparing to confront their doom –
Until they reached the dining room
Where Granny sat as pleased as Punch,
Enjoying a light salad lunch,
And round her, carefully arranged,
Were Grandpa's things. Their faces changed.

'We thought . . . ' George said. 'Well, you thought
        wrong,'
Said Granny, 'I've thought hard and long.
How can it possibly be right
To chuck things that give such delight?'
Said Grandpa, 'I am not a fool;
I knew you couldn't be so cruel.'
She said, 'Don't be too sure, old chap.
The pipes have gone, and so's that cap.'

A Bus Pass Named Desire

The 49 is not a bus that most consider sexy.
If anything, it's one of those that gives them
      apoplexy.
Which goes to show you never know when
      lightning's going to strike you –
A singleton aged sixty-three, and other women
      like you.

The drivers of our buses are a characterless lot.
If they have pleasing qualities, they are difficult to
      spot.
I'd never really looked at one, or had a conversation
In any sort of language, be it English or Croatian.
But when one finds one's left one's stupid Freedom
      Pass behind,
What can one do but beg for help and hope the
      driver's kind?

'I'm only going to Onslow Square,' I sighed. 'I'm
      really sorry.'
'You've got an honest face,' he said, waving a passing
      lorry.
His eyes looked into mine; I fell in love without
      compunction.

Next thing I knew, I found myself approaching
  Clapham Junction.
Not Eros in Olympic form could strike a heart more
  quickly
Than mine was gripped by naked lust; my armpits
  had gone prickly.

He wasn't very handsome and he wasn't quite my
  sort;
He had a little tummy and his legs were rather
  short.
But handsome is as handsome does. He said, 'You
  want a cuppa?'

At my age this was not an opportunity to scupper.
We talked of this and talked of that; he said he was
  divorced.
The conversation flowed with ease; it didn't feel forced.
I said I hoped we'd meet again. He said 'You never
  know.'
I told him I was Cynthia. He said, 'They call me
  Joe.'

That he was only being kind was very clear to me,
And that was ... well ... the end of that, as far as I
   could see.
Another driver took me back and dropped me at
   Olympia.
My thin veneer of *sang-froid* really could not have
   felt skimpier.

But love does funny things to you – the older suffer
   worse;
They say some feel so weird they think it could be
   good night, nurse.
But dying from sheer passion was the last thing in
   my book.
I couldn't wait to catch that bus and have another
   look.

Day after day, night after night, I rode the 49er.
Quite honestly, I might as well have been in
       Indochina.
My Freedom Pass clutched in one hand, I'd climb
       aboard excited,
But every time my hopes of seeing Joe were rudely
       blighted.
From Shepherd's Bush to Battersea and all stops in
       between,
I pressed my pass against the glass of screen on
       screen on screen.
Like Psyche in the Underworld in search of errant
       Cupid,
I travelled through west London feeling very slightly
       stupid.

And then one day I glimpsed him on a passing 211.
Our eyes were locked; the sun came out; I was in
       seventh heaven.
I tracked him down to Hammersmith. 'Where have
       you been?' I said.
'Looking for you. Where else?' he said. 'I gave you
       up for dead.
I'm almost at retirement age – I'm waiting for my
       bus pass.
Let's travel where love leads while there's some sand
       still in the hour glass.'

Next time you see two oldies sitting upstairs on a
    bus,
And holding hands and smiling, they could easily
    be us.
And if life is overtaking you, then I would
    recommend:
Stick out your hand and hail a bus. Who knows
    where it will end?

Old Darlings

The good old Queen
Has good reason to preen
When you consider that Prince Philip
At ninety-four is still hip.

Dear Stephen Fry
Can say goodbye
To a life of non-stop pleasure
Now he's a happily married treasure.

George Clooney
Can get terribly moony.
But he'd never digresso
From a seductive Nespresso.

Dahling Joanna Lumley
Always speaks very plummily
About garden bridges and Gurkhas
And tells stories that are tear-jerkers.

If buttoned-up Dave
Was to suddenly rave,
The vivacious SamCam
Might break into a Can Can.

Beach Bum

I'm not a man who you'd call fit,
Or wants to look good naked.
I'll never be the next Brad Pitt –
There's no way I could fake it.

Mind you, I'm not exactly fat,
And neither's my ex-wife.
I'm slightly plump and that is that,
And I enjoy my life.

Or did until the fateful day
I slipped into my trunks
And dipped a toe in Studland Bay,
Watched by two handsome hunks.

Their pretty girlfriends stood and stared
At my unsculpted figure.
I honestly would not have cared
But for the blatant snigger.

'I'm going to get beach fit,' I said.
My pub mates gave a sigh.
They said, 'You must be off your head.
You? Fit? And pigs might fly!'

I booked into the local gym;
My trainer's name was Grover.
I turned up feeling pretty grim,
And moderately hung-over.

'I need to lose a little weight,'
I said. 'I've no ambition
To be some kind of sexual bait;
My problem's definition.'

'No problem, mate,' he said. 'You'd like
To look good on the beach.

You could be in for quite a hike.
It's not beyond your reach.'

I lunged and squatted, heaved and pressed,
And sweated on the treadmill.
A physical and mental test,
It brought me to a standstill.

I battled on as I'd resolved,
And though my friends all sneered,
The spare tyre round my waist dissolved,
And marble bum appeared.

I gave up pasta, bread and chips;
I even gave up booze,
And found that I had slimline hips –
I booked up for a cruise.

The sun beat down, the sky was blue,
The Caribbean glittered.
I flashed my torso in full view,
And not one person tittered.

All day I chilled around the pool,
And earned some serious glances.
I may be vain, but I'm no fool:
A man must take his chances ...

Some hope – imprisoned in a room,
Redder than cheap red wine.
Plunged deep in chronic sunburnt gloom,
Coated in calamine.

The Northern Line

A lovely old couple called Alice and Ted
Were old-fashioned Yorkshire folk, born and bred.
They lived in a cottage high up on the moors,
Where they kept a few sheep and worked largely
     outdoors.
The best of all husbands, the best of all wives,
They'd never been ill for a day in their lives;
And the day that old Ted was laid low with the flu,
Alice knew without question what she had to do.

When the doctor arrived, Ted was going down fast.
'I am wondering,' she said, 'how much longer he'll
      last.'
The doctor examined him, stood up and said,
'I am sorry to tell you your husband is dead.'
'Are you sure?' Alice said. 'Could there be some
      mistake?'
The doctor looked solemn; his head gave a shake.
Then Ted cleared his throat, and he opened one eye.
'I'm not dead,' he announced. 'I'm not ready to die!'
His wife blew her nose and she said, 'Now, now.
Don't argue, lad. Doctor knows better than thou.'

Summer of Love

Burr and Marguerite are what you might call LCTs,
Which stands for Last-Chance Trendies and affects
    some OAPs.
They looked the part from top to toe in 1967 –
Turned on, tuned in, dropped out, and life for them
    was utter heaven.
They travelled to Haight-Ashbury when everyone
    was there,
And listened to the Grateful Dead, wore flowers in
    their hair.
They worshipped beauty, love and peace – and fun –
    all summer long
In psychedelic union amid the spaced-out throng.
Nobody swung like those two swung in London in
    the sixties,
Fuelled by pot (and quite a lot), like hyperactive
    pixies.
As followers of fashion they were firmly in the van –
Though sometimes it was hard to tell the woman
    from the man.

At all the big rock festivals they rocked and rolled
    all night,
At Monterey and Woodstock, and the good old Isle
    of Wight.

In '69, like butterflies, they flitted in Hyde Park,
Convinced the Stones were better than Johann
Sebastian Bach.

For most of us those days are like a half-
    remembered dream,
And nothing quite as true to real life as they might
    seem.
But, like insects trapped in amber, there are some
    who daren't move on
And, with Burr and Marguerite, live in an age that's
    long bygone.
If Mick can strut his stuff, they say, at three score
    years and ten,
Then we can live and love just as we used to do back
    then.
And summer's lease, to quote the Bard, won't last
    for evermore,
So why not live life to the full as we did heretofore?

They earn some curious glances down at
    Glastonbury each year,
Inspiring funny selfies and the odd ironic cheer.
They get there two days early and they hire a
    modest yurt,
And wander through the swarming crowds, knee
    deep in mud and dirt.
As street cred goes, they looked about as cool as
    Good Queen Bess:
A strange mélange of this and that – a fashion
    bouillabaisse.
A tie-dye shirt, a miniskirt, and knee-high boots for
    her;

Bell-bottomed jeans and glass love beads and
 granny specs for Burr.

Their life is one long love-in and they wouldn't
 change a jot
While they've still got one another and a decent
 stash of pot.

At seventy, they're happier than clams in butter
 sauce;
As far as all their mates go, they're a life-enhancing
 force.
While other couples flounder in this world of
 laissez-faire,
They remain a fine example of a well-adjusted pair.
Their children roll their eyes at every ghastly lapse
 of taste,
But rarely have their parents left them seriously
 red-faced.

Except for once: a day that lives in infamy for all,
And one that those who witnessed it would rather
 not recall.
Out shopping one warm afternoon, while waiting
 for the young,
Burr flopped down on a nearby bench, his legs and
 arms outflung.
His lank hair hung around his face, despite a faded
 band;

An empty Costa Coffee cup was dangling in one
    hand.
The children wandered down the street; they'd met
    some mates from school.
'Oh, there's my dad,' one said. Their friends said,
    'Wow, he's really cool!'

Just then a passer-by saw Burr. She said, 'Don't
    think me rude.'
She dropped some coins in his cup. 'What you need
    is hot food.'

Off Key

For older men a love affair is filled with hidden
       dangers;
And common sense and thoughtfulness can seem
       like total strangers.
When Roger, sixty-five, became the newest love of
       Celia's
(A widow with an interest, like him, in prize
       lobelias),
Discretion was their watchword and their chief
       consideration,
Which, not surprisingly, required some serious
       preparation.

They found a Tudor-style hotel (with spa) just south
       of Dorking,
Where they would meet in secret for canoodling
       and talking.
They never used their real names, or came or went
       together,
And never failed to make a date, come snow, come
       wind, come weather.
Their room was on the second floor, with
       complimentary teasmade.
They'd snack off his ham sandwiches and little
       cakes that she'd made.

Their faculties were sharp as pins, they left no room
       for error;
A chance encounter with a friend was their abiding
       terror.

In retrospect Rog could have checked that on that
       day in June
The room next door had been reserved for
       someone's honeymoon.
If so, he would have realised that the bridegroom
       was a friend –
A fellow horticulturist he'd once known in
       Southend.

Though you may tread as softly as a John le Carré
       spy.
The best laid plans of mice and men can often go
       awry.

The routine was that Celia left and Roger had a
       shower,
And generally tidied up for roughly half an hour.
That afternoon she said goodbye and gently closed
       the door.
Undressed, he headed for the shower and at that
       moment saw
That lying on a table amid general debris
Was not just Celia's purse, but also Celia's front-
       door key.

'Oh, Celia!' he cried and sprang, gazelle-like, in
    pursuit.
He'd forgotten he was naked, so he didn't give a
    hoot –
Until, that is, the door slammed shut behind him in
    the hall,
And there he was without the key – or anything at all.
And no sign of his lover, just one puzzled bridal pair,
She snuggling in her husband's arms, confetti in
    their hair.

'We have met,' Roger said. 'We showed lobelias in
     Southend.'
'That may be so,' the bridegroom said, 'though I
     would recommend
That if you must exhibit, you should aim to be
     polite,
And stick to pretty flowers and not give the girls a
     fright.
Now, if you would excuse us, put that nasty thing
     away,
Since, frankly, we've had quite enough excitement
     for one day.'

Hints for a Long and
Happy Marriage

The Brigadier and Daisy have been married for an
    age.
For decades now the two of them have read from the
    same page.
They've never had an argument or bandied angry
    words;
Soft-spoken and well mannered, they're as loving as
    two birds.

The secret of their marriage lies in duty and routine;
Their mutual respect is something very rarely seen.
Their household runs like clockwork; everything is
in its place.
They always take the greatest care to give each other
space.
They like to dress for dinner and they dine at half
past eight.
They make nice conversation and they eat what's on
their plate.
Their routine after coffee has not changed in forty
years:
The Brigadier rings the bell; his wife gets up and
clears.

Private Lives

Great love tales of history
Are rarely a mystery;
We're privy to chapter and verse.
For Liz Taylor and Burton
You can be pretty certain
Our inquisitiveness was a curse.

For Oscar and Bosie
Things started off rosy,
But, as things went, were never the same.
Angelina and Brad
Were remarkably glad
When they suddenly made her a dame.

Poor Edward and Wallis
Could never find solace
In exile in France or New York;
While Elton and Furnish
Can turn taciturnish
At any loose gossip and talk.

As for Rodney and Doris
And Sandra and Maurice
And millions of lesser-known lovers,
They have no need to feel
Any wish to reveal
What might lie beneath very soft covers.

Like the famous and rich,
There is always a hitch –
Like the time Rodney had quite a fling
With a lady in Boots,
Who was well in cahoots
With two ex-husbands living in Tring.

And as for old Maurice,
Whose half-brother Horace
Had a whole second family in Peckham,
He made friends with a sailor
Who lived in a trailer
And could bend it *much* better than Beckham.

So the next time you pale
As you're reading the *Mail*
Of some film star who treats his wife rotten,
Just remember that Arthur
Who's married to Martha,
Ended up like Titania's Bottom.

After Life

A life insurance man called Fred
Asked Betty, 'When your husband's dead,
Have you an idea what you'd get?'
She said, 'I thought I'd get a pet:
A Border Terrier perhaps.
They're well behaved, those little chaps.
He does his best, my husband Paul,
But *never* comes home when I call.'

Helping Hand

When you're feeling out of sorts
And you're tired of bedroom sports
And disparaging remarks are being made,
All you need's a little boost
To propel you off your roost,
And with luck your form will quickly be displayed.
They say a little mango
Is a sure route to a tango,
And your faith in nature's arts will be repaid.
And a taste of avocado
Will produce the right bravado
For a gratifying victory parade.
If not, try a nice fat oyster
If you're in the mood to roister
And recall the days when you were a young blade.
But watch out for the bad 'un,
As you'll well know if you have had one.
You should be afraid; be seriously afraid.

Tandemania

When John and Jilly got engaged in 1969,
John never looked her in the eye when he said,
>'Please be mine.'

His back was turned, he stared ahead, the ring
>stayed in his pocket;

His mind was on important things – like should he
>change that sprocket?

Jill gazed with love at her fiancé's well-proportioned
>head.

'I will,' she said. 'How long before we get to
>Berkhamsted?'

For serious tandemaniacs, such scenes are not
>surprising;

In cycling circles life can often be uncompromising.

A café stop for tea and cakes may bring them face
  to face,
But on the road, heads down, flat out, each rider
  knows his place:
The captain at the front does all the hard work and
  the steering;
The stoker at the back – in their case Jill – does all
  the cheering.

Romance is accidental, like a gambler's lucky coup,
But true love's bound to blossom on a bike that's
  made for two.
While all too many marriages are casually ditched,
Keen tandemaniacs are unequivocally hitched.

They honeymooned in Germany and cycled down
  the Rhine.
(Their love was consummated in a pub in
  Rüdesheim.)
They bought an ancient BSA with comfy leather
  seats,
And joined a vintage cycling club which organised
  nice treats,
Like picnics in the Surrey woods and trips to stately
  homes,
And gatherings of vintage bikes on disused
  aerodromes.

They shrank from skin-tight Lycra; their idea of
      cycling wear
Was a pullover and anorak, a helmet and a pair
Of trusty corduroy trousers which they tucked into
      their socks,
And retro-looking cycling shoes as comfortable as
      Crocs.

Road races and time trials over fifty miles or more
Are a highlight for some oldies, but for John and Jill
      a bore.
A Sunday morning tootle to a pub near Potters Bar
Aboard their trusty BSA is fun and not too far.

Not so their friends the Bunters, for whom winning
      was their life.
They could have won the gruelling race from
      Edinburgh to Fife,
Had Audrey not disgraced herself by falling fast
      asleep
While pedalling through Dunfermline. Poor
      Charles could only weep.

John laughed. 'I asked him how he knew; he said he
      heard her snoring.'
He added that was probably because she found him
      boring.

But life, as every lover knows, can suddenly turn
        rotten,
And bite the man that tempts cruel fate severely on
        the bottom.
A fortnight later John and Jill rode gently down to
        Woking;
They stayed for tea and spent an hour just gossiping
        and joking.

Jill failed to see the funny side when Johnny lost his
        mind,
And headed firmly back to London, leaving her
        behind.

'I shouted, but you carried on. Till Addlestone,
 you say?
Before it even dawned on you that I was miles
 away?'
John said, 'I'm really sorry. Nothing personal, I
 swear.
The truth is that I take for granted that you're
 always there.'

It may come as no great surprise to learn that Jill
 and John
Have made some simple changes to the vehicles that
 they're on.
The tandemanic mystique has been pretty well
 debunked
Since Jill announced their old machine had been
 abruptly junked.

Their cycling days are still enjoyed – on separate
 machines:
Unmitigated joy attained by slightly different
 means.
Jill told her friends, 'I think you must agree it's only
 fair
That I should see what lies ahead, and not just
 derrière.'

I Remember It Well

Two erstwhile lovers sit at a café table,
remembering old times.
With thanks to Maurice Chevalier, Hermione
Gingold, Alan Jay Lerner and Frederick Loewe.

HE: We met at Tramp.
SHE: No, it was Stocks.
HE: I got the cramp.
SHE: I got some shocks.

HE:	Oh yes. I remember it well.
	I drove you home.
SHE:	I took the bus.
HE:	We flew to Rome.
SHE:	No, Vilnius.
HE:	Oh yes ... I remember the smell.
	That romantic hotel ...
SHE:	More like a B & B.
	I went there with Mel.
HE:	Oh, I thought it was me!
SHE:	I can't believe that you still swear
	That you and I had an affair.
HE:	Well, yes. *I* remember it well.
	I've never forgotten that evening.
SHE:	What evening?
HE:	When we had our first rendezvous,
	And you came to my old flat in Chelsea.
	I feel sure you remember it too.
	You turned up late.
SHE:	I was on time.
HE:	And in a bate.
SHE:	I was sublime.
HE:	Not quite. I remember it well.
	You had a cold.
SHE:	I was right as rain.
HE:	You'd skied in France.
SHE:	I'd been in Spain.
HE:	We played a Stones LP.
SHE:	I was a Dylan fan.

HE: Though not of me?
SHE: You silly man ...
       Oh I remember you
       And your old flat.
       You fancied me,
       And that was that.
HE: Nothing more? I felt sure ... Bloody hell!

Bake-Off, Darling

Not even Coke and Pepsi have enjoyed such
    competition
As Bri and Beryl Gossage did with furious
    repetition.
From the moment that they married they went at it
    like the clappers;
The wonder was they didn't bring in teams of
    handicappers.
When Beryl claimed her family had outspent his on
    presents,
Bri countered by accusing her of blatant
    adolescence.

From then on battle lines were drawn. Whatever the
    occasion,
They'd go to any lengths to bring about the right
    equation.
Their combative behaviour at bridge tables
    everywhere
Meant that no one ever wanted to invite them as a
    pair.
Their rage in TV quizzes would have put the wind
    up Paxman:
Bri would start as Mr Nice Guy and turn into the
    Mad Axeman.

They took up Scottish dancing like a two-man
    Highland warrior,
And no one who encountered them could possibly
    have felt sorrier.
No willow has been better stripped, no Gordons
    have been gayer;
No matter what the latest craze, Team Gossage was
    a player.

Small wonder that the moment they saw Paul and
    Mary's *Bake Off*,
They knew that this was one for them, and it was
    bound to take off.
No need for them to enter – family honour was enough.
What's the point of facing strangers and pretending
    to talk tough

When the competition's fiercest in one's kitchen
       back at home,
And you know that your competitor's a real
       gastronome?
No need to hear Miss Perkins squeaking 'Bake!'
       right in your ear,
Or to suffer degradation when Paul Hollywood
       comes near.

With a contest once a fortnight and their offspring
       as the judges,
They fell upon their mixing bowls and set aside
       their grudges,
And launched into dear Mary's all-time favourite
       cakes and tarts
In the hope of captivating all their teenage
       children's hearts.

They loved their father's brandy snaps and
       Mummy's florentines,
And argued over which was best and caused some
       frightful scenes.
Dad went one up with carrot cake with mascarpone
       topping,
But Mum pulled back with scones and some
       extremely clever shopping.
Her Easter lemon pavlova was obviously a winner,
And Dad refused to say a word throughout the
       whole of dinner.

Next time he scored a triumph with a cracking
      Sachertorte,
But the children were agreed that out of all Mum's
      cakes they thought her
Mango cheesecake on a ginger crust was nothing
      less than awesome.
Through gritted teeth their father muttered, 'Thank
      you, I'd adore some.'

At seven-three to Mum the bake-off prize was
      looking certain:
Another win and that was more or less the final
      curtain ...

How Beryl Gossage could mistake a sugar bag
      for salt
Was inexplicable – it wasn't anybody's fault.

Suffice to say her *îles flottantes* were not a *succès fou*,
Which may well have accounted for the smile from
   you-know-who.

Their baking days are over now; they've given up
   competing.
Life's far too short for kitchen wars and rancour and
   drum beating.
Why jeopardise a happy life with ludicrous
   confections?
They'll only lead to family strife and loss of one's
   affections.

So now they buy their dainties at a cake shop down
   the street –
Patisserie of every kind, as much as they can eat.

But habits of a lifetime die as hard as dandelions,
And no one's natural instincts were more obdurate
   than Brian's.
'I like their sponge,' said Beryl, 'and I love their
   gingerbread.'
'I could have made one better,' Bri said, 'standing
   on my head.'

Brief Encounter

Mrs Hotchkiss was a cougar who frequented clubs
    and bars
In order to meet young men who in her book
    ranked as stars.
Psychologists will talk of older women's lost esteem,
And their fierce determination to reclaim the dating
    scene,
To prove they're still attractive, and adorable, and
    wise.
Or, to put it in another way, hot stuff in young
    chaps' eyes.

Now Hottie (as she called herself) was nothing if
    not blunt;
The moment that she scored, she'd say, 'I want to be
    up front.
I don't want a relationship,' she'd tell the lucky guy,
And, with very few exceptions, he would say,
    'And nor do I.'

So there she was at fifty-nine and feeling
    twenty-two,
In charge of her own life again with raunchy
    derring-do.

The riskier the *mise en scène*, the more it turned her
on.
So when one night in Basingstoke she met a chap
called Don,
And he said, 'Let's go back to mine; my mum and
dad are out,'
She didn't even hesitate; there was no room for
doubt.

'It's only half a mile away,' he said. 'It isn't far.'
'Let's go for it!' She seized his hand and shoved him
in the car.

The double bed was king-size, and so, she found,
was he;
And when she'd had her way with him, he made a
cup of tea.
'Just one more time, I think,' she said, 'and then I
must be going.
I don't know what you do to me, but honestly I'm
glowing.'

'Ooh, this is great,' the young man said. 'I've not
done this before ... '
And as he spoke he heard a cough, and, standing by
the door,
Was someone with a large moustache wearing a
pink bow tie.
She clutched the sheet around her breasts; she
thought that she would die.

'Oh, hello Dad, you've got back soon. This isn't what
    you think.
This is an old friend, Hottie. She just dropped by for
    a drink.'

'I know who Glenda Hotchkiss is,' his father said.
    'We met
At dinner at the Hendersons – Gervase and
    Antoinette.

She runs their local church bazaar, or so she
    proudly claims.
She didn't mention anything concerning adult
    games.
If I were you, I'd get some clothes and give your hair
    a comb;
And while you're doing that, I'll run your lady
    friend back home.'

He came back two hours later, looking pinker than
    his tie,
Which, like his whole demeanour, was decidedly
    awry.

The *on dit* is that cougars never go for older chaps,
But as Hottie told Don's father, 'Don't say never; say
    perhaps.'

The Meaning of Laugh

They say that women love a man who makes them
    laugh in bed;
A sense of humour is one way of proving you're not
    dead.
But humour is a quality that's different for us
    blokes:
A funny woman's one who always laughs at all our
    jokes.

The Invisible Man

Now Rob is quite a ladies' man –
Or, rather, had been in his prime.
But this is now and that was then:
A different world, a different time.

But nothing ventured, nothing gained;
His heart felt young, his head held high,
And for as long as hope remained,
His search for love would never die.

His hair is thin, his jowls sag
Like many older men's jowls do
Who flirt and joke and laugh and brag,
Like soldiers before Waterloo.

At eighty-something Rob is still
Impenitently amorous.
For him there is no greater thrill
Than spotting someone glamorous.

The briefest glimpse of leg or thigh
Rekindles smouldering desire.
A pretty woman passing by
Is quite enough to stoke his fire.

He'll follow one along the street,
As breathless as a year-old pup,
Thinking if only they could meet . . .
And wondering why he can't keep up.

Cruel Cupid laughs at witless fools,
Who push their luck like pimply boys
On holiday from public schools
In Abercrombie corduroys.

But Rob's no fool, he laughs right back;
At his age love's a harmless game.
He may regret his long-lost knack,
But still, he's never lost the flame.

Green-Fingered Love

A garden is a lovesome thing: without love, plants
   won't grow.
They need the gentle, human touch as much as fork
   and hoe.
As children bloom and flourish in the soil of family
   life,
So flowers and plants grow strongly, free from
   anger, fear and strife.
And decent men – like princes – will lead rich and
   fruitful lives
If their love for beauty round them is as great as for
   their wives.

Now Piers and Polly Hooper lived in Brighton in a
    flat
So poky they could hardly breathe, and barely
    swing a cat.
But gardens were their greatest love; and every night
    they'd dream
Of visiting another in the National Gardens
    Scheme.
They went to Chelsea every year, and Hampton
    Court, of course,
But all that they could manage was a window box,
    perforce.
Their horticultural knowledge, though, was frankly
    nonpareil,
And friends would seek their wise opinion almost
    every day.

One year they went to house-sit for the dear old
    Ampersands,
Who felt entirely confident their place was in safe
    hands –
Especially their garden, which they cherished like a
    child,
With its fascinating fusion of the formal and the
    wild.
It was open every weekend in the summer to a
    throng
Of garden cognoscenti, recommended by Roy
    Strong.

The highlight was the Yew Hedge Walk, though
    many loved The Dell,
Where Piers and Polly worked for hours weeding –
    which was hell.
They cleared some beastly undergrowth that swept
    around the pond,
Creating a superb view of the water and beyond.
It paid off in the springtime when the
    rhododendrons blazed,
And the visitors stood open-mouthed and utterly
    amazed.

A letter from the Ampersands arrived from Tuvalu:
'We're thrilled to know you love The Dell as much
    as we all do.
The *Hedychium flavescens* must be at its best right
    now,
And every year its creamy flowers are guaranteed to
    wow.
We brought it from Hawaii and it's really rather
    rare,
But seems to flourish happily in woodland over
    there.
It's our great pride and glory, and we're very, very
    fond
Of the way it seems to flow like gold around our
    little pond.'

The word that Polly uttered is politely called an
    oath.
'And you said it was just a weed!' she screamed. 'Just
    undergrowth!'
'Well, what can you expect,' said Piers, 'if people
    will buy plants
From foreign parts that no one can distinguish at a
    glance?
We could have pulled the whole lot out; we only cut
    it back.
It's bound to grow again, so let's not have a cardiac.'

That afternoon they packed their bags and booked
    on to a tour
Of famous gardens of the East, beginning in Jaipur.
They wrote a cheerful letter to the Amps in Tuvalu:
'The *Hedychium flavescens* was a horticultural coup.
The only thing that saddens us is knowing that,
    next year,
The Dell will be more glorious still, but we will not
    be here.'

The Best of All Possible Worlds

Divorce was not on Barbara's mind;
She wasn't the divorcée kind,
Who picks up husbands here and there,
And worries what she's going to wear
When all concerned meet up in court
And alimony fights are fought.

Her husband Jeff was no Apollo –
A bitter pill she'd learnt to swallow.
She wasn't mad on Theydon Bois,
But liked the trees and lack of noise.
The skies were blue, with one small blip:
She had a rather iffy hip.

So goodbye, tennis at the club
And hello, lunches in the pub
With rather boozy book club chums
And superannuated mums,
Who try (and fail) to walk the line
With Sauvignon-style budget wine.

Now Jeff was something of a prude,
And, frankly, wasn't in the mood
For sharing a domestic life
Of chaos with a half-cut wife.

She gave up booze, but all too late;
One day Jeff gave it to her straight:
'You're not the girl I used to know.
I think it's time for us to go
Our separate ways and start again.
The question isn't "if" but "when".'

His wife was fairly knocked for six
And, not to mention, in a fix.
To what extent was Jeff prepared
To worry how an ex-wife fared?

Would thirty years of married bliss
In his mind be a hit or miss?
Okay, so he was nicely caked;
His hefty income wasn't faked.
But rich men can turn oddly mean
And claim they haven't got a bean
When alimony rears its head
And husbands feel they're being bled.

A friend told Babs, 'You need a brief –
A good one if you don't want grief.
I know a chap who'd fit the bill,
Called Frank. He's absolutely brill.'

Babs met him in the Ritz Hotel,
And instantaneously fell
For Frank's good looks, his wit and charm,
And left soon after on his arm.

Next day they flew to Val d'Isère
(Frank owned a little chalet there)
For fourteen days of snow and sun
And the best sex of her life, bar none.

But all too soon dark guilt crept in,
And crippling thoughts of shame and sin,
And worries about Jeff's wellbeing
Distracted her while she was skiing.

But then he rang. 'I've got good news:
I'm living here in Eaton Mews
With someone who I love to bits.

We met each other in the Ritz.
She'd come to meet her husband there,
But couldn't find him anywhere.
She asked around, but drew a blank.
I think she said his name was Frank.'

When Candide got it off his chest
And said that all is for the best,
He might have had this lot in mind,
For whom life turned out to be kind.
Now Frank and Babs and Jeff and Rose
Are four great friends, as friendship goes.
And since Babs had a hip repair,
They've skied each year at Val d'Isère,
And shared the joys of snow and sun,
And know the greatest love, bar none.

Conversations

An elderly couple were lunching one day
In a seaside hotel near Torquay.
The unseasonal sky was depressingly grey,
And so, as it went, was the sea.

The bookings were down and the place wore an air
Of profound and ineffable gloom,
Which had clearly infected this venerable pair
As they sat there alone in the room.

The sommelier stood by the servery hatch
With a long and lugubrious face
As they toyed with the neighbouring fisherman's
    catch,
Which that morning was haddock and plaice.

Forty-five years of marriage can scale down the
    need
For debate and inspired conversation;
And some couples will plump, like the Venerable
    Bede,
For long moments of deep meditation.

And it came as a bombshell, and some disbelief,
When the silence was suddenly broken,
And the wine waiter twigged with a sense of relief
That the husband had actually spoken.

'Do you realise,' he said, 'that the Forum in Rome
Is as wide as the Golden Gate Bridge;
And that we could accommodate our second home
On one shelf of the world's largest fridge?'

The wife sipped her water and let out a sigh,
And scooped a last pea from the dish,
And said, as she raised tired eyes to the sky,
'Shut up and get on with your fish.'

At the End of the Day

A naughty man was Uncle Jim.
There really was no stopping him
From chasing women far and wide
From Christmastime to Eastertide:
A 'nothing-gain-if-nothing-try' chap –
A sort of one-man Venus fly trap.

The corniest invitations worked,
However much he leered and smirked.
'Come up and see my latest etchings'
Scored high among his hideous lechings.

He misbehaved for years and years,
And drove his wife, Aunt Dot, to tears,
Especially when, at a dance,
He snogged the best friend of my aunt's –
A certain Mrs Baskerville,
Who lived quite near in Notting Hill –
And bagged him as her 'bridge assistant'
(A role in which he was persistent),
And whisked him to the South of France,
And led him quite a different dance.
Dot told him he could pack his bags,
But, as with all such scallywags,
The clouds passed by, the storm blew over,
And Jim was back as Casanova.

The women came, the women went.
(And some of them were, frankly, bent.)
Dot simply got on with her life –
A dutiful and patient wife
Who loved her husband, come what might,
Though suffering the odd sleepless night.

Love ends when one half says it does.
She still experienced the buzz
She'd felt that glorious day they wed,
And that night in the bridal bed,
She wisely played the longer game
And chose not to apportion blame.
She told herself, 'It's only sex.

I'd rather he was mine than ex.
No point in going overboard.
True love will be its own reward.'

One day Jim had a nasty op;
His days of roving had to stop.
And now he's quite content to sit
And read *The Times* and watch Dot knit.
No need to speak or to explain,
Or cause each other needless pain.
Once sex has lost its iron grip,
There's no joy like companionship.

Forget Casablanca

When I look at my life and the times that I've had
In countless exotic locations,
From Tahiti and Tonga to Chile and Chad,
I feel nothing but warm excitations.

Like thousands of couples, we've both had our share
Of romance by a far-distant ocean.
And we'll never forget the hot-blooded affair
That suffused us with rampant emotion.

And now we are older, we'll never return
To those places where life seemed so glittering.
But, like Bogart and Bergman, our hearts will
        still burn,
For we'll always have dear old West Wittering.

Happy Valentine's Day

The pink almond tree
Is a symbol of true love
From St Valentine.